Earth Basketry

SCENE TAKEN AT THE DAN BEARD CAMP, PIKE COUNTY, PENNSYLVANIA

These campers work in the woods procuring their basketry materials from trees. *Left*, boy stripping cedar bark from a log; *left foreground*, boy weaving splint pack basket

Earth Basketry

Osma Gallinger Tod

Schiffer Publishing Ltd

West Chester, Pennsylvania

To my Mother and Father
ALICE HOYT and WILLIAM EDWARD PALMER
who in my youth provided unlimited opportunity to
"go forth under the open sky and list to Nature's teachings,"
this book is lovingly dedicated

First copyright 1933 by Orange Judd Publishing Company, Inc.
Copyright © 1986 by Josephine Del Deo
Library of Congress Catalog Number: 86-61206

Printed in the United States of America
ISBN: 0-88740-076-0
Published by Schiffer Publishing Ltd.
1469 Morstein Road
West Chester, Pennsylvania 19380

This book may be purchased from the publisher.
Please include $1.50 postage.
Try your bookstore first.

MY MOTHER—AN APPRECIATION

When my mother died three years ago on January 10th, 1983, her book on basketry had been in print for fifty years. First published in 1933, it quickly became the standard work of its kind. Daniel Carter Beard, whose introduction to the first edition has been incorporated in every succeeding one, praised the book as a "great work" and lauded the fundamentally educational message "touching on the borderland of the coming new school" which taught the imaginative use of natural fibers found readily in the environment. Daniel Beard was prophetically correct. My mother was then, and remained for her entire lifetime, a remarkable teacher, a compelling proselytizer of the "new school" of teaching which emphasized the development of the intellect and the capacity to interpret, create and control one's life through the education of the senses and training in manual skills. Not too different from the precepts of Maria Montessori, my mother's work was in the forefront of a handcraft renaissance which she pioneered, together with others, in the years just after the Depression.

The first successful expression of her interest in this philosophy was her book on basketry, then titled *Basket Pioneering*. Subsequently, she became a national authority on hand weaving, an interest which occupied the major part of her life. In the last two decades of her very long career, she again returned to teaching basketry and added bobbin-lace to her list of extraordinary skills. As a matter of course, she was capable of executing any craft that came under her purview: she had taught bookbinding, crochet, knitting, embroidery and, when I was yet unborn, built for me a museum quality doll house with every architectural detail perfectly realized.

Of all these many professions, however, I was closest in spirit to her work in basketry, perhaps because it was an integral part of my childhood. I recall waking up in the early hours of the morning, as a little girl, to see the light in my mother's alcove still burning as she refined a drawing for her basketry book. It was the year of the "great depression" and we were hard-pressed. My father, Frank Byron Couch, an Adirondack landscape painter, had died in 1928 and our survival depended on articles my mother wrote for homemaker's magazines such as *McCall's, Better Homes and Gardens, Woman's Home Companion, Country Gentlemen, People's Home Journal, Farm and Fireside,* and the women's pages of *The New York Herald Tribune.* In the course of her life, she published more than 300 of these articles on various craft projects, but, in those days, she sometimes received only $5.00 for a complete article illustrated with her fine drawings. In retrospect, however, I remember this period as one of the happiest times of my childhood. We took long walks in the woods on the mountainside where we lived in Suffern, New York; she made me corn husk dolls; showed me where to position a basket birdhouse; surrounded me with a sense of nature which has remained my sense of place and my sense of myself. I grew up understanding what handcrafts meant to the totality of man, and although I chose writing, not weaving, as a full career, I was very adept at the loom even as a child of six and accompanied my mother throughout my adolescent years on her annual Conferences of American Handweavers conducted across the nation.

The logical outgrowth of all this activity as a teacher of weaving and basketry was a series of excellent books. In addition to *Earth Basketry (Basket Pioneering),* she wrote *The Joy of Handweaving, The Game of Weaving, Handweaving with Reeds and Fibers* (co-author O.H. Benson), *Rugweaving for Everyone* and two small books on bobbin lace plus one on embroidery, *Wool Stitchery (Embroidery in Wools).* Most of these books are still in print today.

Osma Palmer Couch (Gallinger Tod) was an indefatigable worker with her hands and with her heart. Her name, Osma, from the old Norse root, Asmund, means "divine worker with the hands." No name was ever more appropriately given, for she imparted a divine grace to everything she touched and her hands themselves were the most comely and strong women's hands that I have ever seen. Had she become the musician she was early trained to be, she would have melted audiences with the particularly delicate and lyrical touch which she produced on her treasured Steinway. I cannot help but reflect on the loss to the musical world of such a talent which was deflected, after serious study at Juilliard and Wellesley College, toward the pursuit of craftwork; however, the vast fraternity of people she has reached and helped would disagree with this nostalgic regret. Her students adored her. She imparted to them, not alone clear, concise directions, but the confidence to fashion a product that inevitably contained her philosophy of the craft and of life in general.

I did not carry on my mother's teaching. Indeed, I could never have taken her place, for there are file drawers filled with testaments to the inspiration she imparted. A month after she died, she received a letter from N. Gujarat, India begging "your valuable publication, *Earth Basketry,* to make our library rich and its best use at large to our poor people." I sent the book at once as a fitting and symbolic gesture, for my mother would have been thrilled at the prospect of reaching out to poor people in India just as she had been devoted to instructing her poor farmers' wives in Michigan, the handicapped of all ages, the young and the old and all the rest who sought her "midas" touch.

Preparing to write this appreciation, I reread *Earth Basketry* and carefully followed many of her directions to check my memory: were they as I had originally thought-so clear, so free of extraneous matter and so perfectly joined to her sources? I found the book not only affirmative of all the foregoing but astonishingly contemporary. It was and is a timeless work which one may use today to rediscover the nature she drew from in 1932 as she documeted over 100 natural sources for basket making. Her research in The Museum of the American Indian, The Museum of Natural History, The Botanical Gardens of New York and the Smithsonian Institute of Washington was so thoroughly done, it settles into the text with comfortable authority.

My return to *Earth Basketry* was a bittersweet journey, for I found again the little by-ways of my youth and I re-examined many of the baskets which spill out on my living room table, hardly less sturdy for all of their fifty years of use. I realize now that my mother provided me then with every inspiration for a full, creative life using the alphabet of nature to create articles of simple substance for everyday use. As a result, I grew up independent of consumerism, and I have benefitted, lifelong, from a sense of self reliance. The baskets of my youth will undoubtedly end their useful life in my hands, but others that you, the reader, will fashion, will take their place and will renew, not only the skills my mother taught, but her sense of man's divinity through the understanding and appreciation of the natural world.

Josephine Couch Del Deo
Provincetown, Massachusetts
April 20, 1986

INTRODUCTION TO THE FIRST EDITION

This is my workshop, my studio, my study where I write my articles, books, and draw my illustrations; consequently, it is not strange that one may see spilled over my desk, on my easel and heaped upon the floor beside me, working models of log houses, prairie schooners, dog sleds, canoes, dories, noggins, buckskin bags, birch bark pails and hand-made baskets. Most appropriately, nestling in the midst of this medley, are the proof sheets of Osma Palmer Couch's "Basket Pioneering", along with some slender fresh roots, to which bits of the moist humus of the forest mold are still clinging, mixing their earthy tang with the living odor of the fresh roots.

The combined fragrance transports me, like the magic carpet, to the deep, tangled woods where the spruce, pine and woodbine mingle their sweets and at the same time supply free material to those who have the vision to see that from such things beautiful baskets may be constructed. The truth is, the greatest and most useful quality of this book is that it develops the vision of the reader, enabling him or her to recognize the possibilities of the common things, thus making him or her an artisan, an artist, yea, a creator!

All young folks like to make things and the making of baskets is particularly jolly work, because there are few boys or girls who may not become experts. There can be no drudgery in creation. The knowledge that one is of oneself creating something gives one the fine frenzy of the sculptor, the painter, the illustrator, the architect and the author, than which there is no greater joy for child or man.

But the book has a higher purpose than amusement, for the writer, consciously or unconsciously, recognizes the fact that skill with the five fingers cannot be acquired without a corresponding education of the mind. The development of a child's five senses is the development of the intellect which interprets the senses, and this fact will soon be recognized by the new school of educators as the necessary foundation for the work of the kindergarten, grammar school, high school and college. A simple minded person may become a good imitator, but creation develops a vigorous mind totally devoid of inferiority complex. I look upon this book as fundamentally educational and touching the borderland of the coming new school which will produce doers and thinkers in place of parrots, *doers* who, like the early American pioneers, will push forward into newer and more fertile fields of thoughts.

Yes, this author, consciously or unconsciously,
is doing a great work.
All success to
her book.

Brook Lands, Suffern, N.Y.　　　　　　　　　　　　　　　　Dan Beard
1933

AUTHOR'S PREFACE

Some obviously cultural benefits accrue to the child from learning and plying the basket craft. This is true not only of knowledge and skill acquired in fabricating the finished product, but also of the contacts with Nature made in obtaining at first hand the large number of available materials. With a minimum of simple tools—a knife, an awl, and possibly a needle, the child may, with materials native to his own environment, costing but a little effort and perhaps a trifle of carfare or gasoline, intensify and broaden his interest in and knowledge of Nature, train his eye and hand in rhythmic movement, cultivate his appreciation of color harmonies, and develop his sense of the appropriateness of material to purpose, and the adjustment of size and shape to use and place. And the while this profitable and pleasurable process is taking place, he is actually creating something useful and beautiful; he is attaining some of that potential dominion bestowed on man in bending materials to his own constructive purpose, in seeing take form under his own manipulations an article he can enjoy, take some pardonable pride in, and triumphantly give to another as an embodiment, an expression, of his own time, effort, accomplishment, and personality. With all this, too, he cannot but have come to know Nature better, to have a wider appreciation of Her great wealth and beauty and friendliness, to have a desire to gain an ever increasing measure of that understanding of Her constant charm and ready helpfulness that characterized the American Indian, who has passed on to us so much of what he learned in this interesting and useful craft.

The author is deeply grateful to Gene Weltfish for stitches from *Prehistoric American Basketry Techniques* and *Indian Notes;* to William C. Orchard and the staff of the Museum of the American Indian, Heye Foundation, for an unlimited supply of basket types and assistance in photographing; to the American Museum of Natural History for basket pictures; to M.G. Kains and authorities of the New York Botanical Gardens for plant identifications; and to the Crowell Publishing Company for the use of cuts formerly published in *Farm and Fireside.*

Acknowledgment for contributions is due George E. Fowler, G. Meredith Russell, and Mrs. Eli Hunt.

CONTENTS

ILLUSTRATIONS

PART I—ROUND BASKETRY MATERIALS

PART IV—NOVELTY BASKETS

FIGURE 1—IDEALISTIC BASKET-TREE

In the vegetation of every region Nature provides basketry material in abundance

BASKET PIONEERING

CHAPTER I

NATURE'S STOREHOUSE OF BASKETRY MATERIALS

"Such blessings Nature pours,
O'erstock'd mankind enjoy but half her stores."—YOUNG

IF you should visit the countries of the world, you would be surprised by the variety of baskets. Nature grows different plants in different climates, and the basket makers use the fibers at hand: the tough leaf, stem, and root parts, either split into fine strands or left whole. The study of basketry, then, like the study of Nature, is an endless pageant of new delights, offering discoveries in environment, beauties of plant textures, wonders of fibrous strength, and marvels of color. When you have learned basketry, you will at once know how the basket you take in your hand is made, whence it comes, and what are the interests of the people who made it. Possibly you may even be able to name its fibers, to distinguish between the green palm and banana leaves used in tropical countries, the pale bamboo of China and Japan, the flax of New Zealand, yellow orchid skin of New Guinea, tough gray stem fibers of Spain and Algeria, beach grasses of Alaska, brown willow of France and England, or, in our own land, split roots and barks, rushes, fern stems and leaves, as well as imported reed.

Even wider is the variety of basket types, fashioned for particular purposes. The original basket makers are certain birds, especially the African weaver bird and our own Baltimore oriole whose pouch-like woven nests swing high aloft, built to keep the nestlings safe from harm. In baskets are gathered the flowers from hillside and meadow in spring, from gardens in summer. Baskets hold our picnic lunches, and the homely products from farm and market. Special types of baskets add to the attractiveness of window displays in fruiterers', bakers', and delicatessen shops. In the home, tea trays, bread baskets, sewing baskets, scrap baskets and countless others add to our comfort. Beside the fireplace, a basket holds the logs ready to shed forth the warmth and cheer that Nature has stored in them; while near at hand a pet basket invites the cat or dog to curl up cozily, and the work basket awaits the hour of loving labor. The most beautiful basket perhaps, is the gift basket with its store of surprises to cheer the loved one far away, or the lonely heart at holiday time; and last but not least the dainty bassinet to hold baby, who like the birdling, is first cuddled in a basket.

FIGURE 2—Girl scouts creating baskets from materials found on their own camp grounds. Girl at left, weaving a willow tray; girl on rock in foreground, splitting willow rods like an Indian, using her teeth to secure tension; center front, sewing coiled grass basket; right, splitting cedar bark strips from a log. *Top row, left*, shirring leaves from willow withes; *center*, braiding cat-tails for moccasins; *right*, inserting willow buds into a basket border.

CHAPTER II

GATHERING AND PREPARING MATERIALS.

*"He is a thoroughly good naturalist
Who knows his own parish thoroughly."*

HE character of a basket is determined by the kinds of plant fiber used. These fall naturally into three groups, round, flat and flexible. Round rods, such as willow and reed, described in Part I, are generally woven around other stiff round rods called spokes, arranged in a circle like the spokes of a wheel. Flat strips, like ash splints or cane, described in Part II, are more easily plaited in and out of one another, or wrapped and twisted over stiff rods. Flexible strands, like grasses or the fibers of crushed stems, described in Part III, are generally sewed around a center in a coil, then upward in a spiral to form the basket sides.

Gathering Materials—We will make many discoveries of the wonders of Nature while pioneering for basketry supplies. Experience taught the Indians where to find the best fibers. They dug up roots, washed and split them, trimmed trees of unneeded twigs, hammered strips of bark from well soaked logs, pulled and dried clumps of grasses. Basketry materials seem easiest to acquire where Nature has already exposed or discarded them, like the bare roots of trees and bushes where a stream has washed away the soil, water-soaked logs splitting up into their fibers, last year's woody vines beneath the new growth, or shoots at the bases of trees. If we are observing and thoughtful we can gather all our supplies without damaging growing things.

Coloring—The Indians used vegetable dyes to color pale fibers, but often they left the material its natural color, barks brown and gray, roots red and purple, grasses tan and green. Black was obtained by soaking fibers in stagnant water several weeks beside a piece of iron, or by burying strands underground until darkened. We may soak natural fibers in concentrated cloth dyes to get various shades.

Working with Friends—Gives one a chance to exchange ideas. Those fond of Nature may form groups to go pioneering in the greenwood. At home all may join in opening and drying the fibers; then around the garden pool or on a shadowed log beside the brook where a dam of stones keeps the rods from floating away, happy hours of creating await the basket lover.

Tools Needed—Provide a tub for soaking fibers, (if a pool is not available), heavy scissors for cutting, an awl, pliers, a tape measure, and a sharp knife for trimming and splicing. For coiled work you will need blunt tapestry needles.

Care of Baskets—Baskets become brittle and break after a time if they are not cared for properly. Shellacing gives a glossy protective coat, but the shellac should be renewed every year or so. Baskets not shellaced should be soaked in water half an hour or longer once a year. Washing removes the dust and supplies moisture to the fibers in place of that afforded under natural conditions.

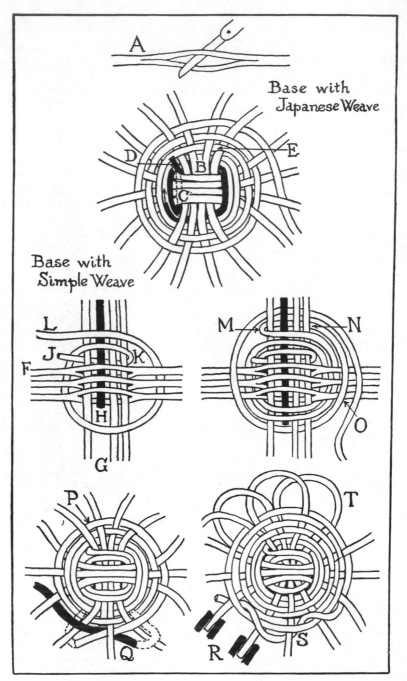

FIGURE 3—SIMPLE BASKET CENTERS WITH SPOKES ARRANGED
IN TWO GROUPS

PART I—ROUND BASKETRY MATERIALS

CHAPTER III

BASKETRY BASES WOVEN WITH ROUND MATERIALS

GENERAL RULES

THE spokes form the basket framework. They must be stronger than the weavers that twine around them, to hold the shape of the basket.

A good base is dome-shaped like an inverted saucer, the basket resting on the outer edge. Therefore use a heavy weave at the edge.

If the base spokes are stiff, insert smaller spokes beside them for the sides.

SIMPLE BASKET CENTERS WITH SPOKES ARRANGED IN TWO GROUPS—FIGURE 3

Base With Japanese Weave—In this base a single weaver ties together two groups of spokes that cross at right angles. Soak eight spokes well. Split four at their centers, A. Insert four others through them, B. Insert end of a fine weaver, shaded, beside whole spokes, C. Carry it upward over split spokes and under its own point, D. Weave clockwise under four spokes and over four, continuing three times around. Then pass the weaver over two spokes and under the third, E, and keep weaving around, "over two and under one." The single weaver comes out at a different spoke each time around, making a weave of close texture. This single-strand weave can be used only over a number of spokes not divisible by three—for seven or eight but not nine, ten or eleven, but not twelve, etc.

Base With Simple Weave—In this center a single strand weaves around an uneven number of spoke ends. Cut six whole spokes and a seventh half spoke; soak well. Split three whole ones, F, at their centers, A. Insert whole spokes, G, with half-spoke, H, between, through split spokes, F, making thirteen ends. Start a fine weaver, J, behind G spokes; pass it back of them to the right, K; reverse to the left in front, pass under end J, down behind F spokes, over G spokes, etc. Weave under and over the groups counter-clockwise, as at L, for two rounds. At M reverse again and weave clockwise under the groups you wove over before, etc. for two more rounds, O. Divide spokes into single ones, P, and weave "under one and over one" continuously. The single weaver comes out at an alternate spoke each time around; the texture of the weave is plaited like wickerwork. Piece weavers behind any spoke, Q. As base widens, insert new spokes, R, separating them into single ones, next page. For a mat, twist weaving end around last row, S, and turn spoke ends down into weaving in loops, T.

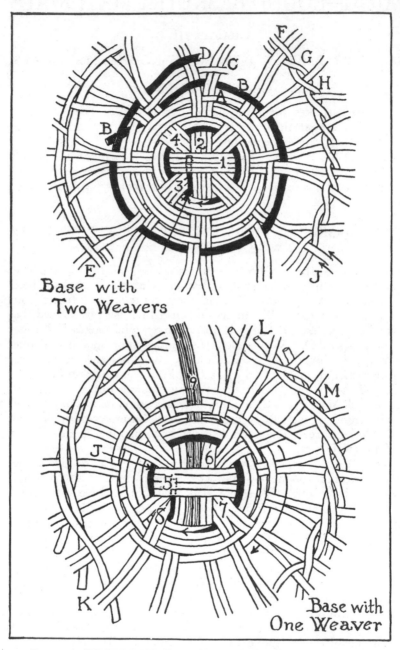

Base with
Two Weavers

Base with
One Weaver

FIGURE 4—INDIAN BASKET CENTERS WITH SPOKES ARRANGED
IN FOUR GROUPS

BASKET CENTERS WITH SPOKES ARRANGED IN FOUR
GROUPS—Figure 4

Sixteen-spoke Basket Base With Two Weavers—In this base four groups of spokes, each having four spokes, cross at their centers, and two weavers alternate in successive rows around them. Lay four parallel spokes (group 1) at right angles to four more (group 2) at their centers. Lay four more (group 3) diagonally underneath them. Lay the last four (group 4) under and at right angles to group 3. Hold groups together between thumb and fingers while a friend ties a string around them (following course of shaded reed at center). Insert weaver under group 1, dotted lines, carry it up under group 3 (see arrow); weave clockwise under and over the groups for three rounds, following track of shaded circle. Then pass weaver under two adjacent groups, bringing it out over a group it went under before; weave alternately over and under the alternate groups for three more rounds.

Divide spokes into pairs, as at A, and weave under and over the pairs once around to C. Insert weaver B (shaded) under the last pair that A went over. With B weave once around to D, stopping one pair at left of C's stop. Continue around with C and stop one pair to left of D's stop, etc. As base widens divide pairs into single spokes, as at E. The spokes may also be separated as at F, by twisting two weavers between them, G and H, (see Pairing Weave, Figure 8). For a wider base insert new spokes, as at J, arrows.

Indian Basket Base With One Weaver—In this base four groups of spokes, each having four spokes, cross at their centers; an extra pair of half-length spokes is inserted in one of the groups to give an uneven number of pairs so that only one weaver is necessary. Arrange groups 5, 6, 7 and 8 like groups 1, 2, 3 and 4 above. Insert the two half-length spokes in middle of group 6, (see grained spokes, 9). Insert weaver under group 5, carry it up under a diagonal group and weave under and over the groups for three rounds. Separate spokes into pairs and weave under and over, following curving arrows. Each time around the weaver will come out at an alternate pair as there are seventeen pairs. To weave in and out in this way with one weaver, always secure an uneven number of spokes or pairs of spokes.

Before turning up base put in a heavy weave at the edge, as at K, (see Triple Weave, Figure 9). For a wider base separate pairs of spokes into single spokes, either with Triple Weave, as at L and M, or with Pairing Weave, as at F.

[7]

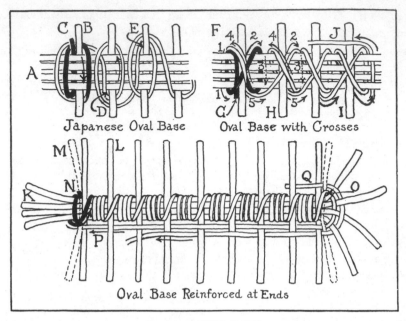

Japanese Oval Base

Oval Base with Crosses

Oval Base Reinforced at Ends

FIGURE 5—OVAL BASES

OVAL BASES—FIGURE 5

Baskets built on oval bases have long narrow shapes convenient to handle, like the narrow market basket carried at one's side, or the oval pack basket fitting against the back.

Oval bases, like round ones, should have their centers a trifle higher than the outer edges. This basin-like shape is given by pulling tighter on the rows of weaving near the edge than on those at the center. Always use Simple or Japanese Weave for oval bases; Pairing Weave twists them out of shape. (See Figures 7 and 8.)

Japanese Oval Base—Short cross spokes are laid under and at right angles to long ones and bound together with the loops of a weaver. Cross long spokes, A, at regular intervals with shorter spokes, B. Start shaded weaver C, end up, beside first cross spoke. Carry it down under long spokes, up over them and in back of its own end to fasten it. Make circuit around first spoke clockwise back to C, passing under both ends of B and over long spokes. Before tying on second spoke, cross weaver over to opposite side, to D, arrow. From D make circuit around second cross-spoke counter-clockwise, passing under both ends of it and over long spokes. When back to D again, cross to next junction at third cross spoke, E, arrow, and from E make circuit clockwise. Continue fastening odd spokes clockwise, even spokes counter-clockwise.

Oval Base With Crosses—In this base short cross spokes, F, are laid over and at right angles to long ones and bound together with the crossings of a weaver. Lay long spokes parallel. Start shaded weaver, G, end down, beside first cross spoke and carry it up over long spokes to starting point of stitch, marked 1. Follow arrow downward under long spokes. Repeat the directions between following asterisks for each cross. * Weave diagonally upward over cross spoke, arrow, 2; straight down under long spokes, arrow 3; diagonally upward to left in a cross, arrow 4; and back to starting point. From here carry weaver diagonally downward to right beneath arrow 4 and under long spokes, to arrow 5, *. Repeat for each cross spoke, as at H, starting all fastenings from same side, 5, arrows. At last cross-spoke, I, start weaving around base with same strand. Use Japanese Weave, J,—"over two and under one" —if the number of spoke ends is *not* a multiple of three; and Simple Weave,—"under one and over one"—if the number of ends *is* a multiple of three.

Wrapped Oval Base Reinforced at Ends—In this base short cross spokes are slit through their centers, long ones inserted through the slits. A weaver fastens them with over-and-over wrappings, taking the same number of turns between each two short spokes. Slit short spokes, L, through their centers leaving ends entire. Insert long spokes, K, through the slits. Add extra spoke, M, beside each end spoke to fill in the end spaces. Insert shaded weaver, N, end up, between short end spokes, wrap it once around long spokes to fasten it, and carry it up over first crossing, dark arrow. Wrap it around long spokes three or more times, then cross to next section and repeat. At point O beyond last short spoke, separate all spoke ends and weave in-and-out clockwise with the wrapping strand. Weave around as at P, completing first round at Q. Here insert second weaver to alternate with first one (see alternate weaving, Figure 4, A to D). Weave until oval is 2 inches wide then change to larger reed for greater strength. Finish edge of oval base with Pairing or Triple Weave, (see Figure 4).

Instead of the single crossings over short spokes shown from N to O, one may use the double crossings shown above, G, H, I.

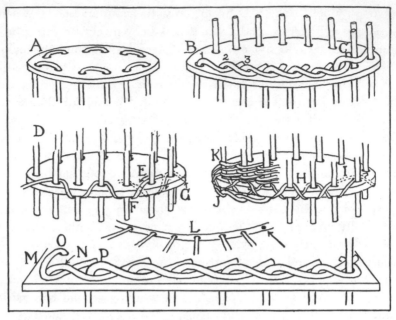

FIGURE 6—WOODEN BASES WITH HOLES BORED FOR SPOKES

WOODEN BASES WITH HOLES BORED FOR SPOKES—
FIGURE 6

Wooden bases are used for the bottoms of serving trays, wood baskets, flowerpot holders, and baskets where a smooth base is desirable. Often beginners prefer to make first baskets on wooden bases. These are convenient for practising all kinds of basket weaves, first inserting spokes in the base, then trying various stitches along the spokes and ripping out the work for more practise.

Wooden bases are often made of veneered board ³⁄₁₆ to ½ inch thick. As this tends to separate if wet the spokes must be soaked well but wiped dry before inserting them in the holes. The holes are bored about ¼ inch from the edge to accommodate spokes of various sizes. Tray bases may be made from thin pieces of well seasoned lumber, the holes bored with an auger. For large wood baskets use board ⅜ to ½ inch thick; if well planed and sandpapered this plain board will do as well as veneered board.

Simplest Way to Insert Spokes in Wooden Bases, A—Cut the spokes twice as long as the height desired, measuring from wooden base to spoke tips, soak well, bend double and insert through adjacent holes, forming loops on under side of base. There must be an even number of holes for this method of inserting. The loops rest on the table to protect the veneered base.

Base With Separate Spokes in Each Hole, B—About 2 inches of the spoke ends project below the base (bottom side up in diagram). Each spoke end is rolled in front of the end at its right and to the inside, as at C. Pass spoke No. 1 in front of No. 2 and back of No. 3. Treat ends toward right thus. The number of holes may be odd or even, but it is best to have an uneven number so that when the basket is turned right side up you may use Simple Weave with one weaver. Bend last end under first loop.

Decorative Stitch to Ornament the Edge of a Wooden Base, D-K—Slip a fine weaver, E, behind a spoke; bring it out over the edge of the base and in behind the next spoke, this time on the other side of the board, as at F; then cross over to first side and pass behind next spoke, etc., until you have woven once around. Continue twisting behind spokes, first over the base and then under it, for a second round. If the number of spokes is uneven, the weaver will come out behind the spokes it omitted before, both above and below, as shown by dotted lines at G, forming crosses, as at H. If the number of spokes is even, you will have to pass behind two spokes at the end of the first round to cause the alternation, as at dotted lines, I. Finish off the lower ends of the base in the usual way, as at J, and start the weaving of the sides above the edge, as at K.

Holes Bored Horizontally into the Edges of a Wooden Board, L—The wooden centers of some cake trays, table tops, footstools, etc., are bored with holes at right angles to their edges, as shown at L, and the spokes are inserted as at arrow.

Square Tray Base, M—Each spoke-end is finished off in the usual way by passing it in front of the end at its right and in behind the second end. Turn the corners as at N: pass the spoke-end just at the left of the corner, O, in front of the corner spoke, N, and behind the next spoke, P. If the corner spoke tends to spring up slightly tack it down with a spraddle tack.

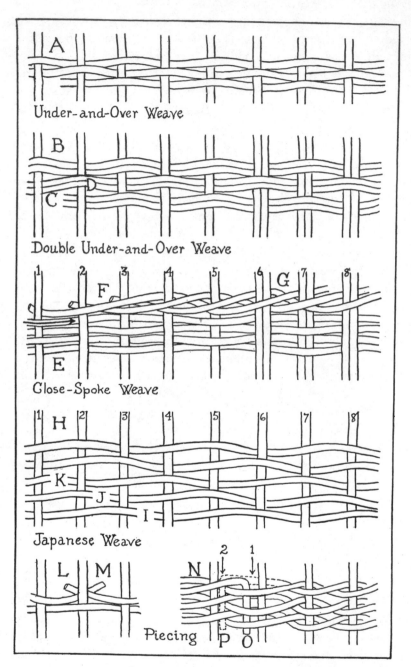

FIGURE 7—WICKER WEAVES

CHAPTER IV

FUNDAMENTAL BASKET WEAVES WITH ROUND MATERIALS

WICKER WEAVES—FIGURE 7

Simple Under-and-Over Weave, A—(Called also Simple Weave, In-and-Out Weave)—The weaver passes under one spoke and over the next. If there is an uneven number of spokes, use one weaver; if an even number, two weavers: pass the first under and over spokes around basket to within two spokes of the start; start the second behind spoke at left of first weaver's start and alternate with its course; continue in successive rounds, stopping each weaver two spokes at left of last weaver's stop, and taking up the latter for next round.

Double Under-and-Over Weave, B—This is the same as Simple Weave with two parallel weavers used as one. If there is an uneven number of spokes, use one pair; if an even number, two pairs, the first started as at C, the second as at D. Double Weave is pretty with double spokes, as at right of sketch B.

Close-spoke Weave, E—When the basket spokes are crowded, use this weave with some spokes left uncovered. The number of spokes must be a multiple of 4, plus 2,—*i.e.* 18, (16 plus 2); 22, (20 plus 2), etc. Pass a single weaver in front of spoke No. 1, (see arrow) and back of next three spokes, Nos. 2, 3, and 4; over No. 5 and back of Nos. 6, 7 and 8. The weaver comes out at the same spokes each time around.

Close-spoke Weave can be used for four or five rows only; then a row of Pairing or Triple is added, as at F, to fasten in the outer spokes, and the Close-spoke Weave continues. It is attractive to use with colored spokes, and over double spokes, as at G.

Japanese Weave, H—A single weaver passes in front of two spokes and back of a third, including three spokes in each stitch. To make the weaver alternate each time around the number of spokes must *not* be a multiple of three. Start the weaver as at I, over spokes 2 and 3, and under spoke 4. In the next row, J, the weaver will come out one spoke to the left, under spoke 3; in the third row, K, under spoke 2. The fourth row is the same as the first. Note the diagonal texture.

Two parallel weavers may be used as one in Double Japanese Weave; and three or four weavers may be used in a group to make a still wider weave.

Piecing Weavers, L—Slip the new end, L, back of the spoke where the old end, M, finishes. For a smoother piecing, N, insert the old end, O, beside a spoke, as at arrow 1; and insert the new end, P, beside the spoke next to the left, as at arrow 2. These piecings may be used for both Wicker Weaves and Pairing Weaves, Figures 7 and 8.

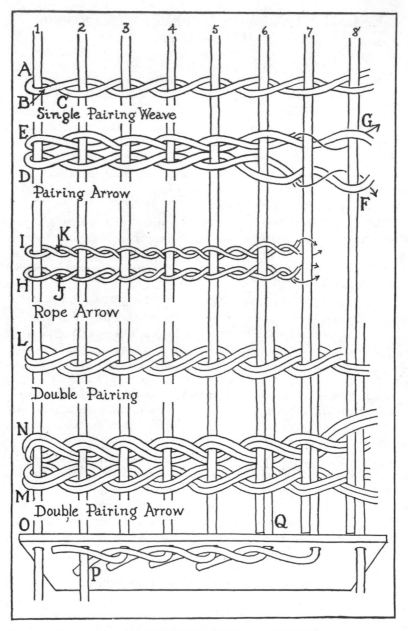

Figure 8—PAIRING OR TWINING WEAVES

Two single weavers or two pairs of weavers are twisted around the spokes and also over each other in between the spokes.

Close rows of Pairing are used to make the water-tight baskets of the Indians; while rows of Pairing with spaces in between are used to make their grain sieves and light carrying baskets. This same method of twining was used to hold the twigs of trees together for primitive shelters.

Single Pairing Weave, A—Insert two weavers in back of two successive spokes, or fold a weaver double and slip its loop over first spoke, as at A. Carry left weaving strand, B, in front of first spoke, over other weaver, C, and in back of second spoke. Carry other weaver, C, which is now at left of B, over spoke at its right, over other weaver, and in back of second spoke at its right. Continue twisting the end at left over the other end and back of next spoke.

Pairing Arrow Weave, D—In this weave there is a regular row of Pairing, D, and a reverse row, E, above it, with the strands twisted in the opposite direction. In row D, bring the left weaver out from underneath the other weaver and cross *over* it, as at F, arrow. In the reverse row, E, bring the left weaver out from above the other weaver and cross *under* it, as at G, arrow.

Pairing Rope Arrow, H—In this weave there is an extra twist in between each two spokes, as at K and J. The weave is used in openwork baskets to keep the spokes evenly apart, as well as to finish off sections of Single Pairing. It prevents sections of weaving next to openwork from slipping.

To make first row, H (often used as a single row) follow rules for Single Pairing at D, and take an extra twist in between spokes in same direction, as at J. To make reverse row, I, follow directions for reverse row at E, and take an extra twist in between spokes in same direction as the reverse.

Double Pairing, L—Two pairs of weaving ends are used together as two single weavers, as at L. Follow directions given under Single Pairing, using two weavers folded double and looped around first spoke, instead of a single weaver.

Double Pairing Arrow, M—Two pairs of weavers are used as two single ones to make the weave shown at M and N. For row M follow the directions for Single Pairing given at A and D; and for row N, the reverse directions given for row E. Double spokes, shown at Q, are effective for this stitch.

Practising Weaves, O—A helpful way to practise various weaving stitches is to insert spokes in a wooden base, fasten their ends below the board, P, and practise weaving over the spokes above the board, O.

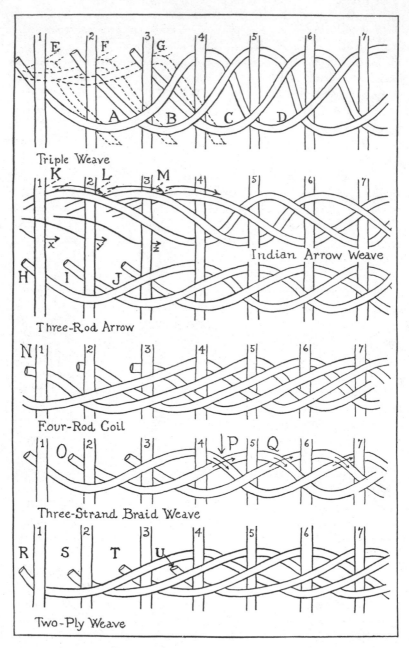

FIGURE 9—WEAVES USING THREE OR MORE STRANDS.
TRIPLE WEAVES. COILS

A Gallery of Earth Basketry

REED WORK BASKET, 12 INCHES DIAMETER CONTAINING
SHREDDED AND COILED SAMSWERIA, FIBER USED FOR
PANAMA HATS, AND PAJA TOQUILLA FROM QUENCA,
EQUADOR, FLORIDA PINE NEEDLES AND BRAIDED CORN
HUSKS.

WORK BASKET WITH SPLINT SPOKES AND TWISTED GRASS WEAVERS. SEE ALSO P. 126, FIG. 61-A.

RAFFIA BASKET BY MOSES FROM MONROVIA, LIBERIA.
THE HANDLE WAS ADDED TO SELL IT AS A POCKETBOOK
TO TOURISTS.

COILED GRASS BASKET, 11 INCHES DIAMETER, MADE BY
OSMA TOD.

WORK BASKET OF COILED GRASSES AND PINE NEEDLES AND STITCHED WITH A PALMETTO WEAVER, 6 INCHES DIAMETER.

REED WORK BASKET MADE OF NO. 3 SPOKES WITH A GROOVE FITTING FOR THE LID AND WRAPPED HANDLES.

FLAT, OVER-ARM CARRYING BASKET MADE FROM A PALMETTO
FROND AND THE HANDLE OF BRAIDED PALMETTO.

REED CUP-HOLDER 3 INCHES HIGH 2¾ INCHES WIDE.

REED FLOWER VASE HOLDER, 4 INCHES DIAMETER.

FLOWER POT CUFF MADE OF A PLAITED MAT AND REED TRIMMING, 6 INCHES DIAMETER. SEE ALSO PAGE 134. FIG. 65b.

REED BASKET WITH A 3-BRAID FLAT BORDER FLAT, 12 INCHES DIAMETER. SEE ALSO P. 28, FIG. 15, MADE BY OSMA G. TOD.

TRAY SHOWING GROUPED SPOKES AS BASE CENTER (SEE PAGE 6, FIGURE 4) WITH TRELLIS BORDER (PAGE 20, FIGURE 11) 2½ INCHES HIGH, 10 INCHES DIAMETER, MADE BY OSMA G. TOD.

CORALBERRY FRUIT BASKET, 8½ INCHES DIAMETER. SEE ALSO PAGE 48, FIGURE 24-A, MADE BY OSMA G. TOD.

REED BREAD BASKET WITH TRELLIS BORDERS — SUPPORTING BASE RIM AND TOP, 10½ INCHES WIDE. SEE ALSO PAGE 20, FIGURE 11.

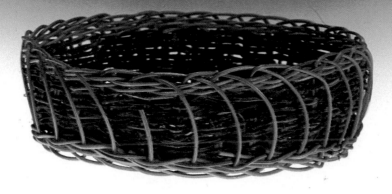

WISTERIA BASKET WITH REED BORDER, 10 INCHES DIAMETER.

FLOWER CONTAINER OF HONEYSUCKLE VINE, 4½ INCHES DIAMETER, MADE BY OSMA G. TOD.

BASKET WITH FLARING CUFF WOVEN WITH DOUBLE WEAVERS OVER TRIPLE SPOKES. 7 INCHES HIGH, 3½ INCHES DIAMETER.

HAND BASKET MADE WITH COMMON CHAIR CANING IN A HEXAGONAL STITCH, 7 INCHES DIAMETER.

HANGING FLOWER HOLDER MADE OF SPLIT BARK, 5 INCHES DIAMETER.

MAT WOVEN FROM PINE NEEDLES WITH SPLIT AND FERN STITCHING. SEE PAGE 54, FIGURE 27, NUMBER 14.

MELON BASKET, 6 INCHES HIGH. SEE PAGE 90, FIGURE 43.

MELON BASKET MADE FROM WOOD
PLINTS, 5 INCHES HIGH, 3 INCHES
DIAMETER. SEE PAGE 90, FIGURE 43.

BASKET TRAY MADE OF LARGE
BUNDLES OF GRASSES AND
STITCHED WITH BARK SPLINTS.

REED MAT SHOWING INDIAN BASKET BASE WITH SPOKES ARRANGED IN 4-PAIRS AS SHOWN ON PAGE 6, FIGURE 4, AND A LOOPED BORDER AS SHOWN ON PAGE 4, FIGURE 3T, MADE BY OSMA G. TOD.

RAFFIA TIED OVER COW HORN WITH KING SOLOMON'S KNOT, SEE PAGE 42 FIGURE 22 AND PAGE 130, FIGURE 63L, MADE BY OSMA G. TOD.

DESK TRAY MADE WITH CEDAR BARK AND CATTAILS BY OSMA G. TOD.

WILLOW BASKET WITH LOOPED BORDER, 11 INCHES DIAMETER.

OVAL, RAFFIA, MARKET BASKET SHOWING THE SPLIT STITCH, 14 INCHES WIDE.

REED FISHING BASKET MADE ON A ONE-SIDED OVAL BASE. SEE PAGE 25, FIGURE 12-A AND PAGE 62 FIGURE 30, MADE BY OSMA G. TOD. BASKET MADE WITH YUCCA LEAF, 6 INCHES DIAMETER.

HAND BASKET MADE WITH
WRAPPED REED AND SEWN
WITH RAFFIA USING A SPLIT
STITCH, 4⅝ INCHES LONG.

SMALL, FINE WEAVE BASKET
WITH ALTERNATING FLAT AND
ROUND WEAVERS AND
BORDER OF PAIRING WEAVE
AS SHOWN ON PAGE 20, FIGURE
11, NUMBER 3, 5½ INCHES OVAL,
OPENWORK BASE, MADE BY
OSMA G. TOD.

WASTEPAPER BASKET MADE OF
REED, CEDAR SPLINTS AND
WISTERIA VINE, 11 INCHES
DIAMETER, MADE BY OSMA G.
TOD.

SCRAP BASKET WITH DOUBLE
SPOKES AND SPLIT BARK
WEAVERS, 11 INCHES HIGH, 6
INCHES DIAMETER, MADE BY
OSMA G. TOD.

BASKET WOVEN WITH GRASSES
AND SPLINTS, 7 INCHES LONG,
ILLUSTRATING THE TECHNIQUE
DESCRIBED IN CHAPTER XIX,
MADE BY OSMA G. TOD.

These rope-like weaves are used to accent the edges of bases, and to separate different kinds of weaving; also for continuous heavy weaving.

Triple Weave, A, B, C—Place three weavers, A, B, C, behind three consecutive spokes, Nos. 1, 2, 3. Carry left weaver, A, to the right, in front of two spokes, Nos. 2 and 3, *over* other weavers and back of next spoke, No. 4. Carry B over Nos. 3 and 4, back of No. 5; C over Nos. 4 and 5, back of No. 6. Repeat, taking left of three strands, D, etc.

Coils—A single row of rope weaving is called a coil. The weavers at the finish must be locked with the starting weavers to give a continuous rope effect.

Three-rod Coil, E, F, G—Finish three weavers, A, B, C, in back of starting spokes, Nos. 1, 2, 3, as at E, F, G. Carry left end, E, beside weaver A, under coil to outside of basket; carry second end, F, beside B, under coil to outside; carry last end, G, beside C, under coil to outside. Trim ends.

Four-rod Coil, N—Place four weavers back of four consecutive spokes, as at N, Nos. 1, 2, 3, 4; carry each left one in turn to the right in front of three spokes and back of fourth. To lock coil, finish four weavers back of four starting spokes, then carry each under coil and out to front beside its initial weaver.

Five-rod Coil—Place five weavers back of five consecutive spokes; carry each in turn in front of four spokes and back of one, or in front of three and back of two. Finish coil by passing each weaver under coil and out to front beside its initial weaver.

Three-rod or Indian Arrow Weave, H-M—By adding a reverse coil above a regular coil the opposite weavers meet in arrow points. *Regular Coil*—Weave one round of Triple Weave starting three weavers, H, I, J, behind spokes Nos. 1, 2, 3. Finish weavers back of their starting spokes, K, L, M, dotted lines. Bring K, L, M to outside of basket, passing each in turn on top of weaving and in front of next spoke, curving arrows. *Reverse Coil*—Pass left weaver K in front of two spokes at its right, Nos. 2 and 3, *under* other two weavers and back of third spoke, No. 4. Repeat with each weaver. To finish reverse coil, pass first end, X, back of its starting spoke, No. 1; next end, Y, under coil and back of spoke No. 2; third end, Z, under coil and back of spoke No. 3.

Four- and Five-rod Arrows—Add a reverse four- or five-rod coil above a regular coil.

Braided Triple Weave, O-Q—Carry each strand, as O, over two spokes, Nos. 3 and 4; before passing under third spoke, No. 5, cross it under preceding weaver coming from behind spoke at this point, arrow P. After this crossing carry weaver behind third spoke, No. 5, where it in turn is crossed under by next weaver, as at Q.

Two-ply Weave, R-U—Place four weavers, R, S, T, U, behind four consecutive spokes; carry each left one in turn to the right, in front of two spokes and back of two.

Piecing Rope Weaves—End old weaver behind a spoke. Hold it out away from spoke toward inside of basket. In space thus made between old weaver and spoke, insert new weaver, shove its end to left along old one, bring its long end out to right, and continue weaving.

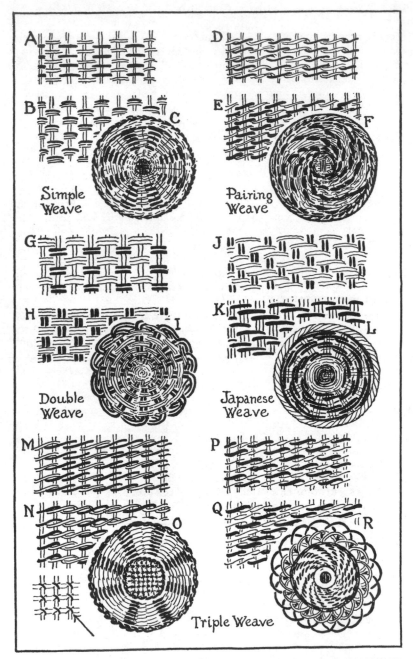

Figure 10—MATS AND PLACQUES OF VARIOUS COLORS AND TEXTURES

CHAPTER V

COLOR AND TEXTURE IN DIFFERENT WEAVES—
FIGURE 10

EAVING stitches vary greatly in their textural nature, some mottled, some ribbed, others with continuous spiral lines. You can emphasize these effects by using two different weaving materials or two colors of the same material, such as strips of dark bark with white ash, red and tan grasses, etc. Pairing and Simple Weave, with two weavers, admit of two colors; Triple Weave admits of three; while in Double Weave and Japanese Weave you may use spokes of one color and weavers of another.

Color in Simple Weave, A, B, C—To obtain vertical straight lines of color, A, use Simple Weave with two weavers of contrasting color over an even number of spokes. To obtain a mottled effect, B, use two weavers of different color over an odd number of spokes. The round mat at C has a column design, with two colors over an even number of spokes.

Color in Pairing Weave, D, E, F—Pairing Weave with two different colors, like Simple Weave, results in vertical columns with an even number of spokes, D; and in a spiral, with an odd number of spokes, E. The mat at F has an odd number of spokes and is woven with two contrasting pairing weavers, making a spiral.

Color in Double Weave, G, H, I—To obtain a column effect, G, weave with two pairs of spokes, each pair a different color, over an even number of spokes. Two pairs over an odd number brings four weavers over the same spoke. Additional contrast in color is obtained by using spokes of one color against weavers of another color, H and I.

Color in Japanese Weave, J, K, L—Use spokes or pairs of spokes of a contrasting color to the weaver. At J, weaver is lighter than spokes; at K and L, spokes are lighter than weaver.

Color in Triple Weave, M-R—For straight vertical lines, M and N, two spokes are of one color, the third of a second color, and the number of spokes is divisible by 3 (12, 15, etc.). For a spiral upward to left, P, the number of spokes when divided by 3 leaves a remainder of 1 (13, 16, etc.); for a spiral upward to right, Q, the number of spokes when divided by 3 leaves a remainder of 2, (14, 17, etc.). For a mottled effect, the three spokes are of three different colors.

In mat at R, the double open border is made by adding a second set of spokes of a second color. The center of mat O, arrow, has interlaced spokes, their crossings tied together with raffia or rush.

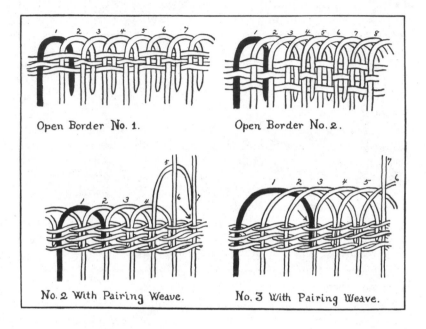

Open Border No. 1.

Open Border No. 2.

No. 2 With Pairing Weave.

No. 3 With Pairing Weave.

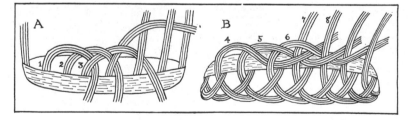

FIGURE 11—*Above*, OPEN BORDERS. *Below*, TRELLIS BORDERS

CHAPTER VI

BASKET BORDERS

ASKET borders are made by turning down and finishing off the spokes in various ways. There are three kinds: open, closed or rolled, and braid borders. Choose a border for your basket that will correspond in size and style with its weaving. If the spokes seem too far apart, insert others and finish with pairs of spokes, or carry a weaving strand along with the spokes to fill in and strengthen the border. Soak spokes thoroughly to prevent their breaking and to render them pliable enough to twist into a snug finish.

OPEN BORDERS—FIGURE 11

Open borders are made by bending the spokes over one another in loops. Of a lacy appearance, they are splendid for mats, fancy vases, cake trays and flower-pot covers.

Open Border No. 1—Measure the length of loop desired and trim spokes to this length. Bend each spoke over in a loop and insert its end down into the weaving beside next spoke at its right.

Open Border No. 2—Bend each spoke over in a loop, skip first spoke at right and insert end down into weaving beside second spoke at the right.

Open Border No. 3—Bend each spoke over in a loop, skip next two spokes at right and insert end down into weaving beside third spoke at right.

Trellis Border—The spokes are interlaced to form openwork. Pass spokes in group 1 over group 2, under group 3, and down over sides of basket, as at A. Carry each group "over a group, under a group and down." Turn basket upside down, as at B, and make border at bottom of basket as follows: Carry group 4, over group at right, 5, under next group, 6, over next group, 7, and in behind next group, 8. Carry each group in succession "over a group, under a group, over a group and in."

Trellis borders at the bases of baskets form supporting rims. If a top border, A, and a bottom border, B, are separated by wide basket sides, the groups of parallel spokes form attractive curves over the sides, especially lovely if the spokes are colored. The groups of spokes may be interlaced in various ways. Another border follows the rule, "carry each group under a group, over a group, and under a group to the inside." See cake basket, Figure 25.

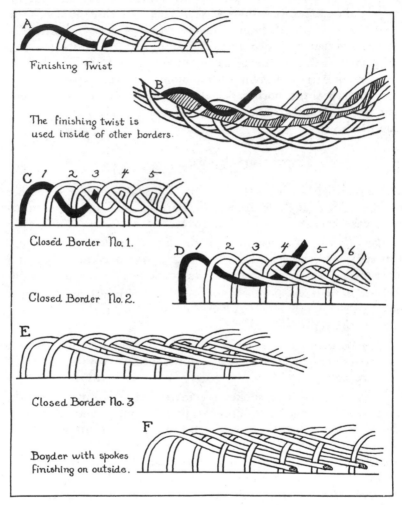

A

Finishing Twist

B

The finishing twist is
used inside of other borders.

C 1 2 3 4 5

Closed Border No. 1.

D 1 2 3 4 5 6

Closed Border No. 2.

E

Closed Border No. 3

F

Border with spokes
finishing on outside.

FIGURE 12—CLOSED BORDERS

There are many kinds of closed borders. The simple ones, A to C, should be used
for narrow finishes; the heavy ones, D to F, for wide outstanding edges.

In closed borders the spokes are twisted or rolled over one another and their ends locked firmly beneath the border. The simplest type of closed border is a single turning of the spoke-ends over one another, in the Finishing Twist, A, B. It may be used alone as a border, or it may be added at the inside edge of other borders to fasten their ends. In more substantial borders the spokes are twisted in and out of several others, C-F.

Simple Finishing Twist, A—Carry each spoke-end, as shaded spoke at A, in front of end at its right and in back of second end at right to inside of basket. The rule is, "over a spoke and in." The finishing twist is used at the inside of other borders to fasten spoke-ends, as at B.

Closed Border No. 1, C—Carry any spoke, as shaded spoke No. 1, under spoke at its right, No. 2, over second spoke at right, No. 3, and to inside of basket. Repeat in succession as each spoke becomes left spoke. The rule is, "under a spoke, over a spoke, and in."

Closed Border No. 2, D—Carry each spoke in succession, as shaded spoke No. 1, under spoke at right, No. 2, over second and third spokes at right, Nos. 3 and 4, and to inside of basket. The rule is, "under a spoke, over two spokes, and in."

Closed Border No. 3, E—Carry each spoke in succession, as first spoke at E, under spoke at right, over next three spokes at right, and to inside of basket.

These closed borders afford many variations. Each spoke may pass under several spokes, over several, and in; or over one, under one, over one and in; or over two, under two, and out to front of basket to form a rustic border with the spoke ends cut on the outside, as at F. Try out various combinations for your basket, selecting that which seems suitable to the basket texture.

Rolled Closed Borders—Carry each spoke in succession over several spokes at its right and to the inside of basket. To fasten spokes inside of this rolling stitch, use the Finishing Twist, A. A rolled border was used for the top edge of fishing basket, just beneath lid, Figure 12-A.

Wrapped Borders—A wrapped border consists simply of a single flexible strand wrapped round and round a foundation rod, as shown at the edge of the fishing basket lid, Figure 12-A.

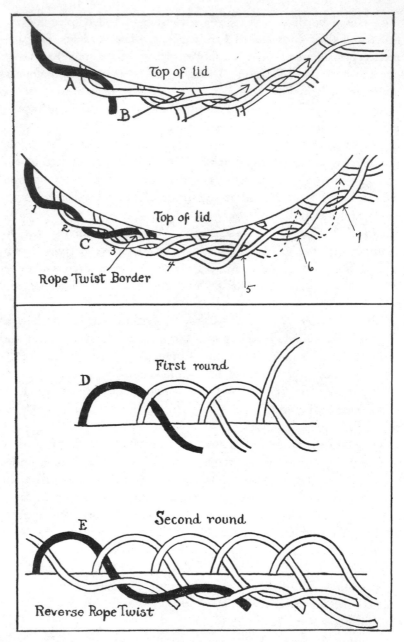

Top of lid

A
B

Top of lid

1
2
C
3
4
Rope Twist Border
5
6
7

First round

D

Second round

E

Reverse Rope Twist

FIGURE 13—DOUBLE TWISTED BORDERS

Rope Twist Border, A-C—Consists of a repetition of one simple stitch, forming a closely-bound rope-like edge, especially suitable for fine baskets or the edges of basket lids. With the lid turned right side up and its edge toward you, carry each spoke in succession in front of next spoke to right and out, as at A, shaded spoke. Do this to all spokes around basket. Now following direction of arrow at B, carry shaded spoke over two spokes lying just at right and behind next spoke to inside of border, to conceal each spoke-end. The finished rope begins to take form at C with spokes tucked in as at dotted arrows. After all spokes have been concealed, the Finishing Twist may be added at the inside.

Reverse Rope Twist Border, D-E—Is a double finishing twist that forms a rope-like edge on the outside of a basket; with its ends clipped outside, it is effective for rustic baskets. Twist the ends under the ends at their right instead of over them as in regular Finishing Twist. First step:

Figure 12-A—THE LID OF THIS FISHING BASKET HAS A *WRAPPED* BORDER, THE BASKET PROPER, A *ROLLED* BORDER. DIRECTIONS FOR MAKING BASKET, FIGURE 30

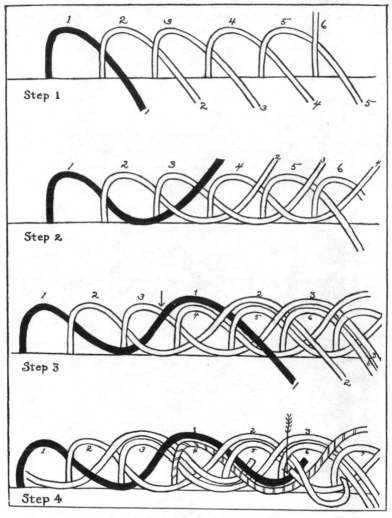

FIGURE 14—SIMPLE UPRIGHT BRAID BORDER

carry each spoke in succession in back of spoke at right and to outside, as at D. Second step: twist each spoke-end in succession over spoke-end now at right, then under it to outside of basket, as at E, shaded spoke.

BRAID BORDERS—Figures 14 and 15

Braid borders are both strong and beautiful—a double incentive to master them. Parallel strands cross and recross rhythmically, moving forward in a wave-like procession of curves, and the spokes are so intertwined they cannot possibly slip out. Braid borders should be mastered step by step.

Simple Upright Braid Border, Figure 14—This border stands perpendicular to the bottom edge of a basket. It is splendid to use for baskets viewed from the side, like hanging baskets or fruit and flower baskets.

Step 1: Carry each spoke in succession, as shaded spoke No. 1, back of spoke at right, No. 2, and to outside of basket.

Step 2: Carry each spoke-end, as shaded spoke No. 1, in front of second spoke at right, (No. 3) under spoke coming out at this point, (No. 2) and over curving part of same spoke just passed over, (No. 3). Repeat with each spoke.

Step 3: After spoke has passed over this curve, as at vertical arrow, carry it parallel to next spoke, (No. 4) under next end, (No. 2) also under spoke this lies next to, (No. 5) and to outside of basket. Treat each spoke in succession in same way.

Step 4: Carry spoke-end, shaded, that has just come to outside of basket, parallel to same spoke to which it was parallel in Step 3, (*i. e.,* striped spoke No. 4) and pass it over next two parallel spokes, (Nos. 3 and 6) to inside of basket, as at feathered arrow. Treat each successive spoke the same, pull all ends taut and trim on inside.

Rapid Braid Border, Figure 15—This imitation braid border is convenient to use when the spokes are in pairs or close together; it is like the Simple Braid Border in appearance. When the spokes left for a border seem too few, insert other spokes beside them and use this border.

To make Rapid Braid Border, carry a pair of spokes, (or two adjacent spokes as shown here) to right in back of next pair of spokes, (or next two adjacent spokes) in front of next pair, (or next two) and to inside of basket. In Figure 15 Nos. 1 and 2 go under 3 and 4, over 5 and 6 and to inside. The rule is, "carry two spokes under two, over two and in."

Flat Braid Border, Figure 15—This horizontal border, lying flat on top of the basket edge, is excellent for all kinds of trays, scrap baskets, footstools and baskets viewed from above.

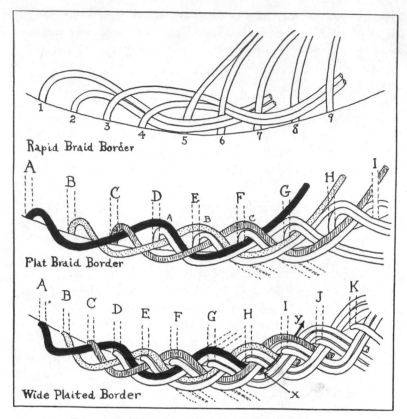

Rapid Braid Border

Flat Braid Border

Wide Plaited Border

FIGURE 15—THREE BRAID BORDERS LYING FLAT

Soak spokes thoroughly. Bend out toward you any two adjacent spokes, A and B. Cross left one, A, over right one, B, and in between next two spokes still standing, C and D, dotted lines; then bring down left standing spoke, C, across A. There are now two spokes out and one in. Cross left one, B, of two outside, over other one, C, and in between next two standing spokes, D and E; then bring down left standing spoke, D, across B. There are now two spokes inside and two outside. Bring left inside spoke, A, down next to and parallel with right outside spoke, D. A and D now travel to outside together. Cross left outside spoke, C, over these two and in between next two standing spokes, E and F; then bring down left standing spoke, E, across it. Bring left inside spoke, B, down next to and parallel with spoke just brought down, E. B and E now travel to outside together. There are now two pairs of spokes outside and a single spoke, C, inside. Cross left outside pair, A and D, over other pair and in between next two standing spokes, F and G. Lay down left standing spoke, F, across them and bring down inside spoke, C, parallel with this one. C and F now travel outward together. From now on repeat directions between asterisks *, all around basket.

* There are now two pairs of spokes outside and one pair inside, as shown by dotted lines. Cross left outside pair (B and E) over right outside pair (F and C) and in between next two standing spokes (G and H) and bend left standing spoke (G) down over this pair. There are now two pairs of spokes on inside. Drop short strand (A) of left pair and lay long remaining spoke (D) parallel to standing spoke (G) just brought down. There are now two pairs outside and one pair inside just as at start of repeat. *

Repeat directions between * until all standing spokes have been bent down. At this point carefully pair ends left with spokes of start, slipping them under and over spokes and parallel to single ones already in place. The course of each spoke is made clear by the preceding one.

Wide Plaited Border, Figure 15—This is like Flat Plaited Border with each spoke braided along a little farther, making three parallel spokes on the inside of braid; effective for large trays, window baskets, ferneries, reed tables and seats.

To weave the border follow directions for Flat Braid Border up to beginning of repeat. At this point first spoke, A, has reached seventh spoke, G, which has not yet been turned down, and there are two pairs of spokes outside and one pair inside (see dotted lines). Carry left outside pair, B and E, over right outside pair, F and C, and in between standing spokes, G and H. Bend down left spoke, G, over pair, and also lay pair A and D down parallel with it, carrying all three to outside of basket. As each standing spoke is brought down, lay left inside pair parallel with it in this way instead of dropping one of pair as in Flat Braid Border. When there are two groups of three spokes each on outside and a pair of spokes on inside use following repeat between *.

* Let drop shortest strand of left outside group, which is strand on the inside, arrow X, and carry two remaining strands over other group and in between next two standing spokes. Lay left standing spoke down over these two strands. Lay left inside pair down parallel to spoke just laid down. * Repeat directions between * all around basket, then adjust remaining spokes beside spokes they would naturally follow. Soak spokes to prevent breaking.

If wider braid still is desired, with groups of three spokes on both inside and outside, carry all three spokes of left group on outside of basket at beginning of repeat, over other group of three spokes and to inside of basket, and drop shortest spoke of group there, as shown at arrow, Y.

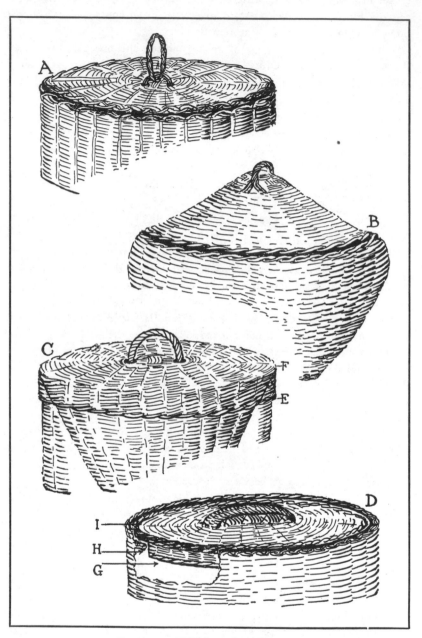

FIGURE 16—TYPES OF BASKET LIDS

CHAPTER VII

BASKET LIDS—FIGURE 16

ASKET lids should be smoothly and closely woven, of the same texture as the basket, and of such form as to complete the basket contour.

Their edges should be carefully adjusted to fit the basket border. Lids may be any shape, round, oval or square, woven according to the same general plan as the basket base. The spokes of the lid should be the same thickness as the side spokes of the basket so the lid border will match the basket border; and the weavers of the lid should be about the same size as those of the basket so the two textures will be similar.

Fitting a Lid to a Basket—Just where the weaving of the lid should stop so its border will fit neatly within that of the basket below depends upon the width of the border used and upon the size of the spokes making it. A careful adjustment is necessary. It is a good plan to stop weaving the lid, without cutting off the weavers, when its diameter measures a trifle less than the inside diameter of the basket border. Then soak the lid well and try its border. If it does not fit, undo it, and either take out or add one round of weaving until it fits perfectly.

Flat Round Lid, A—This lid fits into the border of the basket. A surface of smooth weaving with a uniform stitch makes it an attractive cover for a basket. Finish it with a Closed Border, Figure 12, or Rope Twist Border, Figure 13. Before adding handle, wet the lid and lay it flat on a table under a weighted board so it will dry flat.

Dome-shaped Lid, B—This lid is planned to carry out the graceful curves of the basket beneath. Weave the crown carefully, shaping it by pulling on the weavers with an even tension. Use a simple stitch similar to that of the basket sides. Occasionally place lid over basket to guide its shaping.

Lid with Turned Down Sides, C—This flat lid has sides turning down over the basket edges, at a right angle if the basket sides are vertical, or at a sharper angle if the basket has an outward flare. Weave the lid large enough to cover top of basket, soak spokes well, then tie lid down over top of basket with raffia, tying ends of raffia under basket. Bend spokes of lid down over basket sides and complete the weaving of sides of cover. This is a sure way to make a cover fit. A lid made over outward flaring sides must have a narrow turnover to slip off easily.

Lid with Collar, D—This lid has an inside collar, G, that holds it firmly within the basket ledge H, a horizontal shelf made just inside the basket border. The top edge of the lid, I, slips down into

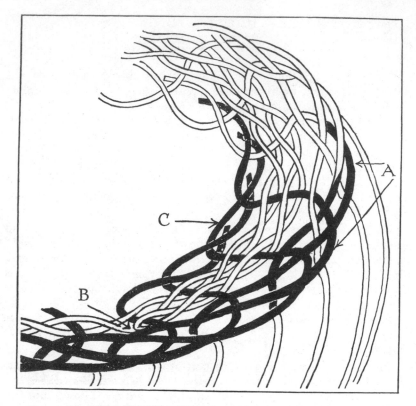

FIGURE 17—SHELF WOVEN INSIDE A CLOSED BORDER TO SUPPORT
BASKET LID

the ledge so the surface of the lid is flush with the top of the basket. This lid is described in detail with diagrams in Figure 31.

Lid with Wide Rim—The lid in Figure 32 has a wide rim jutting out over the basket sides.

Lid with Open Border—A lid with sides like type C may be finished with an open border to match the open border of a basket.

Lids with Straight Sides—Straight-sided lids, either square or oblong, are made by interweaving a flexible strand back and forth between spokes laid parallel on a board. The method is that used in Figure 33, G.

Shaped Lids—A lid may be made any shape by weaving it around a flexible rod, as described for the lid of fishing basket in Figure 30 and Figure 12-A.

Basket Groove for Lid, Figure 17—It is possible to weave a little shelf or ledge inside of the basket border for a lid to rest on. There are three simple steps to follow.

[32]

First step: Put a regular closed border on the edge of basket so the spokes will end up on the inside, as at A, border and spokes shaded.

Second Step: Bend these spokes horizontally toward inside of basket, and, using them as regular spokes, start Simple or Pairing Weave around them with a fine weaver, as at B. Weave two or three rounds.

Third Step: Finish off the spoke-ends by twisting each one over the end at its right in the Finishing Twist, Figure 12. Pull spokes taut while still damp so that ends will dry firmly in place. Make the finished groove from ½ to ¾ inch wide.

CHAPTER VIII

BASKET HANDLES—FIGURES 18 TO 20

IT IS a delightful feeling to carry a basket knowing that the handle is secure and will hold a basketful; and it gives one still keener enjoyment to know that the basket has been made and the handle of it fastened in firmly with the strong confident fingers of the owner. Anyone who has used baskets a good deal knows that they usually give way first at the handle, making them quite useless unless one knows how to mend them. To enable one to make durable handles on new baskets, and to mend the weak handles on old ones is the object of this chapter.

Suggestions for Making Basket Handles—The handle should be in proportion to the basket, and its height and curve should carry out the lines of the basket. It should be stout enough to carry the weight put upon it, yet not too thick to be heavy looking. The worker should be careful to fasten handle-ends securely at the basket sides. When a handle arches above a basket, there should be an even number of basket spokes so the two handle-ends will be exactly opposite. When weaving the top part of a basket with handle, insert short ends of reed the same size as handle reed to make grooves for it, as at Figure 18, A; it is easy to weave around these. Soak the handle reed, bend into its final shape, tie with string and let dry, as at B, so it will not spring outward and make the basket bulge.

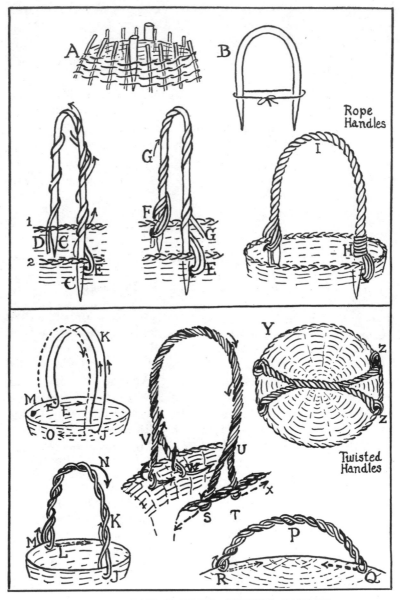

FIGURE 18—ROPE HANDLES. TWISTED HANDLES

ROPE HANDLES—Figure 18

A rope handle is made of a thick foundation rod with a long fine winding weaver twisted rope-fashion around it. Whittle the ends of a well soaked rod to points and insert into basket sides, as at C. Insert winding weaver, D, beside rod on side 1 and wind upward around rod, letting the weaver adjust itself to the size of the rod. At opposite side 2, insert the weaver from outside, as at E, pull strand taut, and wind back around rod, coiling close beneath each first coil, as at arrows. When back to side 1, insert weaver from outside in same hole as start, as at F, and wind upward making a third coil, as at G. Continue coiling between sides until all spaces are filled, as at I. Any piecing should take place at ends of handle. To fasten coiling at each side make a collar of fine reed wound round and round, as at H.

TWISTED HANDLES—Figure 18

Twisted handles are made of several reeds of the same thickness twisted together. Reed sizes Nos. 2, 3 and 4 are best to use. Soak all reeds well.

Twisted Handle of Three Strands, J-O—Measure a reed three times as long as final handle, and allow several inches extra for fastenings. Insert reed into basket below border, as at J, and draw ⅓ of its length through. Twist the ⅓ and the ⅔ ends together above basket, as at K in both diagrams at left. At second side insert short ⅓ end from outside, as at L, and finish off in weaving. Insert ⅔ end from inside, as at M, and twist it back in groove of first two reeds, as at N. At first side, J, end it off in weaving, as at O.

Short Twisted Handle, P-R—Short curving handles, like P, are used for the lids of baskets. Insert a reed at its ⅓ to ⅔ division at Q, twist both ends over to R, finish off shorter one and bring back long one in first groove, finishing it off at Q.

Double Twisted Handle, S-X—This handle has forks at each end. Measure two reeds, each three times as long as final handle. Insert separately at ⅓ of their length at short distances apart, as at S and T. Twist the two ends of each together until four strands meet at U. Twist all four together, unshaded reeds, to V, opposite U; separate into pairs again with a long and a short end in each pair, and twist down to border, opposite S and T. Insert short end of each pair from outside and finish off in weaving, as at W; insert long ends from inside and carry upward to outside, along grooves, shaded arrows, to meet at V. Carry both long ends as a pair back over arch of basket along groove to other side at U; then separate them, carry each down to border in groove of fork, and fasten off, as at X.

Double Twisted Handle for Lid, Y-Z—The handle at Y is a short double twisted handle used for the lids of large baskets. Make as just described, inserting reeds at their ⅓ divisions at Z.

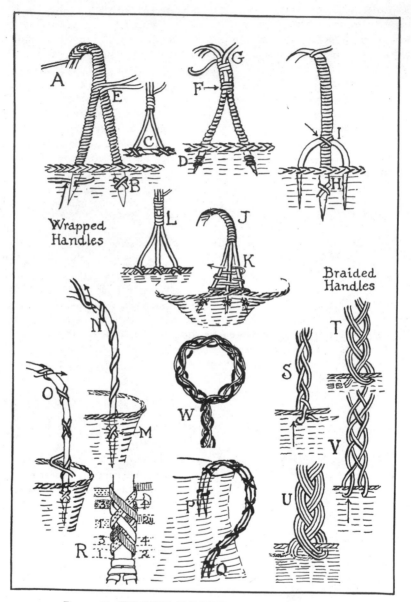

FIGURE 19—WRAPPED HANDLES. BRAIDED HANDLES

A fine weaver is wrapped continuously around one or more thicker foundation rods, Figure 19, A-L, to make a solidly wrapped handle.

Simple Wrapped Handle, A—Insert two whittled rods into basket, as at B; run a long fine weaver through a hole in each rod and fasten with a cross B, or two stitches around border, C. Bring weavers out behind handle and wrap rods, A, closely up to E. Join weavers; wrap them side by side around both rods to opposite fork. Separate rods, wrap each down to border, run weavers through holes in rods and fasten them as on first side. Two short stitches, D, may also be used for fastening.

Decorative Wrapped Handle, F—Wrap two rods as just described, up to fork, lay a third rod over them, its under side whittled flat, wind around all three several times, F; lift top one up and wind around lower two several times, G. Make alternate sections in this way as far as fork on opposite side; cut off third rod and finish wrapping as on first side.

Wrapped Handle with Bracing Rod, I—A single wrapped handle should have a supporting rod at its base, as at H. Fasten main rod, insert curved supporting rod whittled at ends. Wrap main rod up to crossing at I; fasten with a cross around both rods, arrow, and continue wrapping to other side.

Wrapped Handle with Three Rods, J—Bore holes near ends of three whittled rods; insert same distance apart. Run wrapping strand through hole of left rod, tie it to basket with a cross, pass to hole of next one, fasten with cross, fasten third one in same way. Bring winding strand to *inside* of border; weave in and out of rods, as at K. Join rods near top; wrap to opposite side; separate and finish like first side. The rods are sometimes wrapped only across top, L.

Partly Wrapped Handles, M-Q—Fasten rod, as at M; wrap upward at even spaces, N; fasten at opposite side. To make crosses, O, wrap back over handle in reverse direction; fasten weaver to first side. Two parallel rods may be covered with crosses, as at P. Fasten rods at base of handle, Q, coil upward from left to right; fasten at other end, P; coil back from right to left.

Plaited Wrapping, R—Lay a fine strand under handle rods at their fork, ends 1 and 2 (or use strands from wrapped fork). Lay a second strand above first, ends 3 and 4. Cross No. 1, spotted, diagonally to right; cross No. 2, striped, over this to left; cross both ends under rod and bring out above their start, at 1 and 2. Cross No. 3, shaded, to right, and No. 4, white, to left; then cross both ends under rod and bring out at upper 3 and 4. Plait pairs alternately to opposite side; conceal one pair in weaving, wrap two ends of other pair around fork rods to border.

Three-strand Braid, S—Cut a strand a little longer than handle arch, fasten end in border; cut a strand twice as long, loop double over border, as at arrow. Braid to opposite side. Fasten ends.

Double Three-strand Braid, T, and Triple Three-strand Braid, U—Are made like Three-strand Braid with groups of strands.

Four-strand Braid, V—Use two strands, loop double over border, arrow.

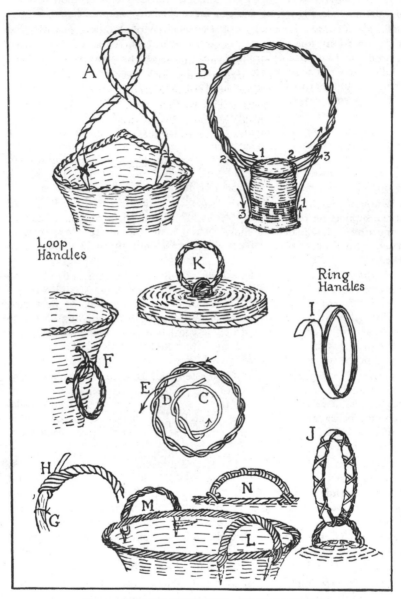

Figure 20—LOOP HANDLES. RING HANDLES

Novelty loop handles offer variety to the usual overhead arch, and small loop handles at the sides of baskets are sometimes more convenient than the larger kind. Ring handles may be coiled, twisted or wrapped.

Loop Handle with Pairing, Figure 19, W—Loop a strand double and attach to top of basket, twist two ends upward to base of loop, W. Here twist them once around in a circle and interlock them through their own strands at base of loop. Now twist them a second time around circle using a pairing twist at right angles to first twist, each stitch locking around that beneath, see shaded strands. Bring strands back to base of circle, then continue interlocking down to basket. A braid may be treated in the same way.

Twisted Loop Handle, Figure 20, A—Twist handle-rod in a loop, and insert ends into basket. Fasten first end into weaving with a cross of winding weaver, as at arrow. Wrap upward across intersection, up over loop, down across intersection again, and down to fastening of rod at second side. The winding reed may reverse to make crosses if desired.

Overhead Loop Handle, Figure 20, B—This circular handle is made of a single long piece of reed. Fasten its end at base of basket, 1, carry upward in overhead arch from right to left, and insert into top of basket at left side, arrow 1. Carry through to point opposite in border, at 2. Make second round twisting reed around first round, and finish in border at left, arrow 2, an inch or two from arrow 1. Carry reed under border to first side again and circle upward in third round, winding reed along groove between first two rounds. Finish at arrow 3 at base of basket opposite start.

Twisted Ring Handle, Figure 20, C-F—Begin with a circle of reed, C, twist reed around it in a second circle, D, and twist it around in a third circle in the groove made by first two rounds, E. Fasten handle to side of basket by a smaller twisted ring passing through weaving of basket, F.

Wrapped Ring Handle, Figure 20, G, H—For sides and lids of baskets. Whittle a thick rod diagonally across ends, splice and tie them, G. Wrap rod closely with a fine strand, inserting end at finish back under last few rounds and drawing them taut.

Coiled Ring Handle—Coil a flexible strand around a spliced rod at even intervals, and continue coiling beside first coils until all spaces are filled. (See Figure 18, G.)

Ring Handles of Flat Reed, I-K—Wrap a long flat strand around over itself as at I. Wrap a flexible strand or some twisted raffia around this with coils going one way; then reverse with coils going the opposite way forming crosses, J. Fasten ring to basket with a twisted loop, J, or a circle of plain reed, K.

Small Loop Handles, L-N—These are small overhead handles. The handle at L is made like a rope handle, that at M, like a twisted handle; that at N, like a wrapped handle. (See Figures 18 and 19.)

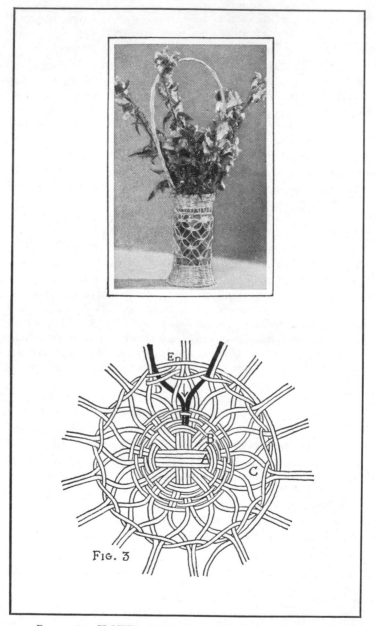

FIG. 3

FIGURE 21—FLOWER VASE OF HONEYSUCKLE VINES.
Below, OPENWORK BASE

CHAPTER IX

BASKETS OF FINE VINES

"Woven into almost impentrable thickets—by the pliant and twisting garlands of the wild honeysuckle."—Miss Mitford.

SOME of the vines that twine about tree trunks, ramble over stone walls or cover our porch trellises, are excellent basket material. Honeysuckle, wisteria, clematis, and many other fibrous vines, provide us with flexible weavers of attractive color tones. Shoots stocky enough to use for spokes, and tendrils suitable for the finest of weavers are to be had.

HONEYSUCKLE VINES

Long flexible one-year shoots of uniform size cut from the vines that grow wild or cling to our porches, may be used unpeeled to make brown woodsy baskets, or with the bark removed to make ornamental baskets of creamy white color and waxy texture.

The vines may be gathered at any time during the year. The largest and strongest, found at the end of the growing season, may be gathered in fall or winter. Remove the leaves and boil the cut vines for three hours with a little concentrated lye added to the water to toughen them. After boiling, clean the bark from the vines by rubbing them with a cloth, and shave off any knots with a sharp knife. Rinse the vines and use while still wet, or dry and hang in bundles until needed. Soak in water before using.

A list of vines similar to honeysuckle will be found at the end of the book.

FLOWER VASE OF HONEYSUCKLE VINES—
FIGURES 21 AND 22

Slender vines or reed are used over a substantial glass jar to make this trellis-work basket with openwork base.

Materials—Spokes the size of No. 1 or 2; weavers, No. 0 or 1; (see footnote); handle, No. 4; jar about 6 inches high.

Base—With sixteen spokes of fine vine or No. 1 reed, 40 inches long, start a center of four groups of four spokes each, as at Figure 21, A. With a fine honeysuckle strand, weave under and over the groups several times. Divide spokes into groups of two; insert two extra spokes 20 inches long shown shaded black at arrow; this gives an uneven number of pairs to weave around with a single weaver, as at B. Weave until central section measures about 1½ inches across, fasten weaver, then cross spokes in space ½ to ¾ inch wide, as at C. Bring spokes together again by

FOOTNOTE—A table of reed sizes is given in Figure 75, end of book. These same sizes are applied to vines, etc., in following basket directions.

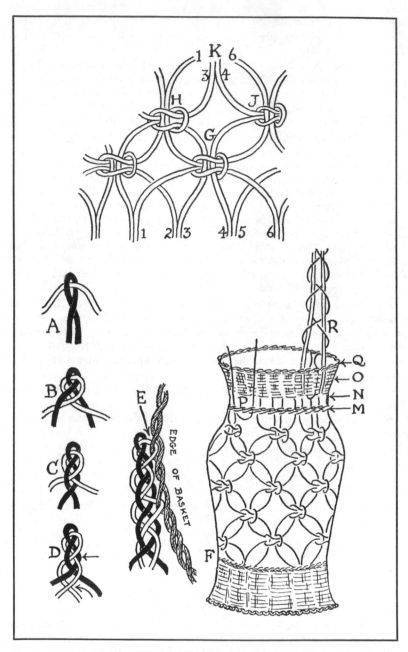

Figure 22—DIAGRAMS OF HONEYSUCKLE FLOWER VASE. *Above*, KING SOLOMON'S KNOT. THIS IS USED FOR TYING FLEXIBLE VINES OR WITHES INTO A LACE-LIKE MESH; ALSO FOR MAKING KNOTTED BAGS OF RAFFIA OR GRASSES

starting Pairing Weave with vine folded double, as at D, and weave once around. Cut off one of pairing weavers, as at E. Continue weaving in and out of groups of two with other weaver until base is a little larger than bottom of jar.

Sides—Soak spokes, turn upward, and weave four rounds of Triple Weave. Cut off two of the weavers, insert jar and gradually pull weaving snugly around it, using remaining weaver under and over the pairs until this section at base of sides, Figure 22, F, measures 1½ inches. Finish band with Pairing Rope Arrow, Figure 8, which holds weaving snugly in place.

Fancy Braid Edge—Leave weaving of sides to add following attractive braid at edge of base, Figure 22, A-E. (Practice edge separately before applying.) Soak two strands of vine, thickness of No. 2 reed, bend each double, then twist one, shown dark at A, around other, shown light. Now twist light around and at right angles to dark, as at B; then twist dark around light, as at C; and light around dark again, as at D. Continue to alternate. Always twist each pair in same direction, see arrows at D pointing to light strands, right side always over. When you have mastered this edge apply it to basket, as at E. Start in same way with two strands, but catch one of strands at every other twist around a weaver at edge of basket, as shown by light strand at arrow, E. Continue all around basket.

Continue up sides with trellis-work which is a succession of King Solomon's Knots, Figure 22, top diagram. This is simply a square knot with two strands tied around two other strands. To make the knots come out evenly reduce number of spokes used to a multiple of four. At F there are thirty-four spokes. Reduce these to thirty-two or twenty-eight.

King Solomon's Knot, Figure 22—For tying knot use spokes six spokes apart, Nos. 1 and 6. Of four spokes between them, Nos. 2 and 5 are not a part of knot but are bent away to be tied in adjacent knots. Tie Nos. 1 and 6 around 3 and 4, as at G. For first half of knot, lay right strand 6 over Nos. 3 and 4; and left strand, 1, under them; then form a half knot. Reverse for second half and lay left strand, 6, over Nos. 3 and 4, and strand 1, now at right, under them; finish knot. These two steps make complete knot. For knots above G, at H and J, carry Nos. 3 and 4 to left and right and use them to tie over other strands in next row of knots; and carry Nos. 1 and 6 to left and right and use with others to be tied over. At K, bring Nos. 1, 3, 4 and 6 together again in a knot similar to G. The tying goes quickly after the start. Keep tying knots up to neck of jar, M. At this point draw spokes together in two rows of Pairing. Leave an unwoven space across narrow neck, N; then start Simple In-and-Out Weave over pairs of spokes, as at O. If you need more spokes for top flare, insert spokes folded double through pairing, as at P.

Border—Just above top of jar at Q, separate spokes into single ones, soak well and weave Closed Border No. 2, Figure 12.

The Handle—Is made of two strands of vine size No. 4, 26 inches long. Whittle ends to points and insert into top band of weaving about one inch apart, down as far as N. Around these wind a well soaked strand, as at R, folding it double and starting looped end under weaving at N. Bring both ends out at border and cross them over handle continuously to other side of basket; insert them into weaving and fasten securely.

[43]

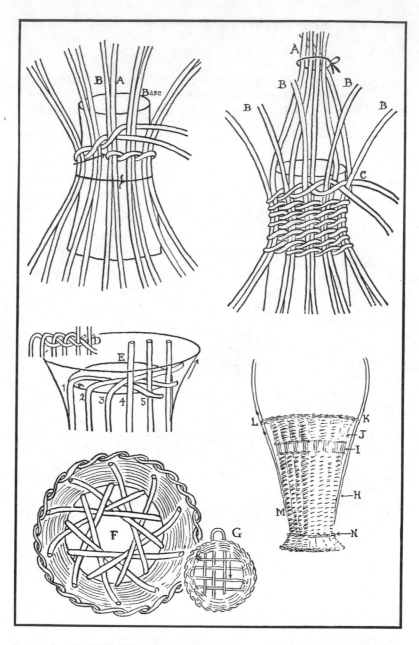

Figure 23—BASKET VASES MADE OVER GLASS BOTTLES. THIS METHOD OF TYING SPOKES AROUND A GLASS JAR AND STARTING WEAVING AT THE TIED PORTION, MAY BE USED FOR JARS OF ANY SHAPE OR SIZE. THE SIDES MAY BE LEFT UNWOVEN WITH THE GLASS SHOWING THROUGH, THE SPOKES CROSSED IN TRELLIS-WORK.

Vases woven over glass bottles may be made attractive by applying the general principles given here. Cut spokes of No. 3 reed (or vine) 10 inches longer than bottle, arrange in pairs 1 inch apart around bottle with 5 inches of the spokes extending below glass bottom, and fasten the pairs around bottle with a cord, as in Figure 23, upper left sketch, basket shown upside down. Start pairing slightly below center, see arrow, using a weaver finer than spokes. Call spokes at right of each pair, A spokes, those at left, B spokes. As weaving approaches base of bottle tie all A spokes together, upper right sketch, and continue pairing around B spokes only, as at C, gradually making an outward curving flare for several inches. Finish edge of flare with Closed Border No. 1, middle sketch, D, carrying each spoke under spoke at its right, over second and behind third.

The A spokes are used to form base for jar to rest on, as at F. Soak spokes well. Bend each A spoke down over glass base, as at E, and under three spokes at its right: carry spoke 1 under 2, 3 and 4; spoke 2 under 3, 4, and 5, etc.

Turn basket right side up and follow weaving shown in basket at lower right of Figure 23. Weave sides in any weaving stitch, as at H, leave space unwoven, as at I, weave section J to top, and finish top, K, with closed border, D. Cut handles of thick reed, insert their whittled ends into weaving at L and M, then tie them down with a pliable strand of No. 1 inserted through hole in handle rod. Also bind handles to border at top of basket with fine strands.

Another way to make a platform for jar to rest on is shown at G. In this case all spokes are used to weave the supporting flare of base and a fine weaver darns back and forth at narrow part of basket, N, above base, making firm platform for jar. Fasten ends of weaver securely.

Note that wherever the weaving changes its direction, as between base flare and sides, at N, the change is definitely marked by a coil of larger weavers. This is true also of the dividing line between two different kinds of weaving, as between open and closed weaving at I, where a row of heavier weaving marks the change. This artistic emphasis is a mark of good basketry design. The shape of the bottle being covered will suggest an interesting pattern for the sides.

FIGURE 24—THIS FRUIT BASKET OF CORAL-
BERRY RUNNERS HAS A DELICATE WAXY
TEXTURE YET STRONG STRUCTURE

FIGURE 25—TRELLIS BASKET FOR CAKE
OR FRUIT

CHAPTER X

BASKETS OF COARSE RUNNERS AND SHOOTS

"The eugh, obedient to the bender's will;
The birch, for shafts; the sallow for the mill."—SPENSER

CORAL-BERRY RUNNERS

THE coral-berry, also called Indian currant and buckbush, is a rough looking bush growing about three feet high, bearing clusters of small white flowers in the summer that turn to red berries during the fall. It sends out runners along the ground that provide a weaving material stronger than honeysuckle vines and as durable as reed or willow. Coral-berry runners are especially practical for large substantial baskets in daily use.

The vines may be gathered any time from August until the sap rises in spring. The bark is slightly scraggly, the color light brown. They make pretty rustic baskets with bark unpeeled; when peeled they have the same waxy finish and cream color as honeysuckle. To peel them, boil in water for three hours; then, using a cloth, push or rub off the bark and trim away the knots with a sharp knife. When vines are clean, dry and hang them in a dry place. Before using, soak them in water an hour to render pliable.

VIRGINIA CREEPER (FIVE-LEAF IVY)

The long runners of Virginia creeper found close to the ground, make baskets of a beautiful deep brown, and their roughnesses add a pleasing texture. Gather the one-year old runners at any time from spring until late fall. Soak them an hour before working. Use the thicker vines for spokes, the finer for weavers. Piece weavers by adding narrow end of new vine to narrow end of old; or, if vine finishes at thick end, start new vine at its thick end.

The woodsy-looking hanging basket marked No. 8 in Figure 27 was made of Virginia creeper, over a small jam jar. It has a Sixteen-Spoke Base, Figure 4; sides of Simple Weaving, Figure 7; Closed Border No. 2, Figure 12; and Three-strand Braid Handle, Figure 19, reinforced with wire. The stems of five-leaf ivy are marked at intervals by nodes. Guard against ·breaking these by soaking runners until very pliable.

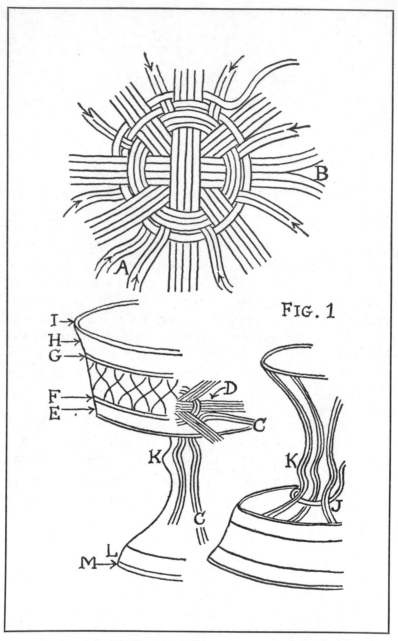

FIG. 1

FIGURE 24-A—DIAGRAMS OF CORAL-BERRY FRUIT BASKET

This fruit bowl of delicate waxy texture is yet strong and durable. Dyed wine color, maise or grape purple, it would blend with the colors of fruit. It is lovely too left its natural color and shellaced.

Materials—Spokes, coral-berry or other strong vine, reed or willow, size No. 4. Weavers, size No. 3.

Upper Base of Bowl—Cut sixteen spokes of No. 4, 30 inches long. Start a Sixteen Spoke Base, Figure 24, upper diagram, weaving under and over groups of four with No. 3 for several rounds. Cut eighteen spokes 27 inches long; insert these in pairs between the groups of four, as at arrows. Insert ninth pair beside eighth, as at A, to give uneven number of pairs to weave over with a single strand. Carry half the length of each inserted pair down through upper base to form base or standard below it, as at C and D, lower diagram. Tie these lower spokes together while weaving flat base of upper bowl part. Weave flat base passing alternately under and over groups of four and groups of two, as in upper diagram, until there is room to separate groups of four into pairs, as at B, making twenty-five pairs. Then weave under and over pairs with a single weaver until base measures 6 or 7 inches across. Finish with a round of Triple Weave.

Sides—Soak basket well; bend pairs upward. With one weaver put in 1 inch of Simple Weave, as at E; one row of Pairing, as at F; a 1-inch section of criss-crossed spokes followed with a row of Pairing, G; and ¾ inch of Pairing flaring slightly outward, as at H.

Border—The border at I is Closed Border No. 2, Figure 12.

Base Standard—Turn basket over. With single strand of No. 3, weave under and over nine inserted pairs, as at J. Make slight bulge at K, then flare spokes gently outward to broad base standard. To fill widening gaps, add two spokes at every pair but one, a spoke at each side of pair, and separate groups of four thus made into pairs, making seventeen pairs. Weave in and out until ½ inch from the bottom, then weave three rows of Triple, as at L, and finish with Closed Border No. 2, M.

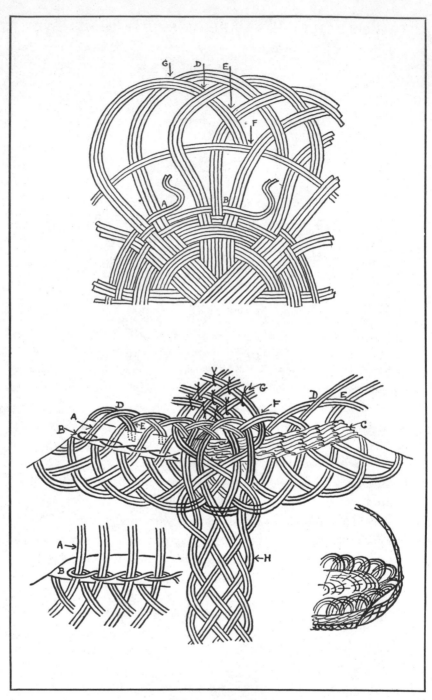

FIGURE 25-A—DIAGRAMS OF TRELLIS BASKET

Few things give the hostess more pleasure than an attractive service for afternoon tea. The beauty of this tray lies in the interlaced weaving of border and handle.

Materials—Spokes of fine willow, honeysuckle vine, or reed, size No. 3. Weavers, No. 3. Handle, No. 3.

Base and Sides—Cut thirty-six spokes 40 inches long, group as in upper sketch like a Sixteen-Spoke Base, Figure 4, but with nine spokes in each group instead of four. Weave under and over groups of nine four times around, alternate with four more rounds, then divide spokes into groups of three. Weave under and over groups with two strands of No. 3 in Double Weave, as at A, and insert second pair, B, to alternate with pair A. Slope weaving gently upward like a shallow saucer until base measures 7 or 8 inches across.

Border—Intertwine groups of three spokes in a trellis border. Pass each group of three over group at right, upper diagram, C, under second group at right, D, over third group, E, and under basket base, F. Make loops extending 2½ inches from edge of weaving. Turn basket over with groups upright, lower diagram, A. Bend a well soaked strand of No. 3 double; pair around groups, as at B, for 7 rows, about 1 inch. This section, lower diagram, C, makes a rim for basket to rest on. Finish off groups of three with following border: pass each group under group at right, as at D; over second group, as at E, and down behind Pairing Weave, as at dotted lines.

Handle—Prepare six groups of three spokes each, 40 inches long, for braiding. Insert groups through successive openings in border, lower diagram, F. Interlace ends and tie them with raffia or string to under side of basket, as at G. Now braid long ends into fancy figure eight between lower rim and trellis edge, as in small sketch, lower right. To close figure eight, insert groups through trellis border edge and start braiding, as at H. Braid strands into an arch 8 inches above basket. Insert groups through trellis border at other side, interlace them in a figure eight, and carry ends through bottom border. Tie groups to weaving under basket. The basket without its handle makes a useful round trellis tray.

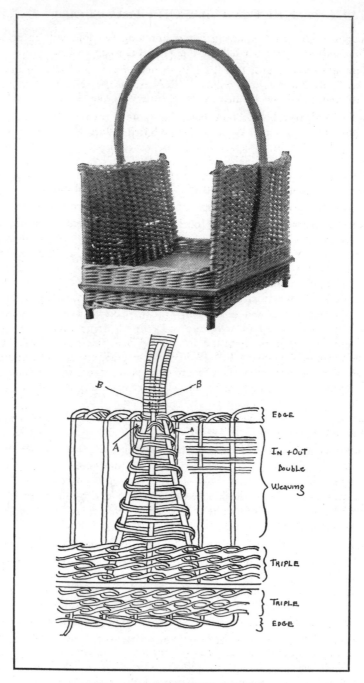

EDGE

IN + OUT

DOUBLE

WEAVING

TRIPLE

TRIPLE

EDGE

FIGURE 26—FIREWOOD BASKET

FIREWOOD BASKET—FIGURE 26

Everyone who needs a strong basket for long fire logs will appreciate the low ends and strong handle of this practical wood basket.

Materials—Base board, 18 x 12 x ½ inches. Four posts 12 x ½ inches. Spokes, ½ lb. No. 5 reed or willow. Weavers, No. 4. Handle, five pieces No. 10 reed, or willow ¼ inch thick; for winding, No. 3.

Base—Sandpaper board; bore holes for posts 1 inch in from corners; glue posts in holes with 2½ inches below board. Bore ³⁄₁₆ inch holes for No. 5 spokes, 1¼ inches apart and ¾ inches from edge of board. Insert forty No. 5 spokes 33 inches long, with 10 inches below board. Turn basket over and weave three rounds of Triple with No. 4 below board, regarding posts as spokes. Add Closed Border No. 2, with Finishing Twist on inside, Figure 12.

Sides—Turn basket up; weave four rounds Triple with No. 4. For low end borders treat left five of eight end spokes as follows: carry each spoke under spoke at right, over second and third, under fourth. Of remaining three spokes, pass left one under spoke at right and out; second one, under spoke at right and out, third one, behind post and out. Use these three spokes in Triple Weave along sides to get to second end, weaving with left one, over two spokes and under one, treating post as a spoke; continue with Triple Weave to post at second end. Finish first weaver, over post, over spoke at right of post and in; second one, under post, over two spokes at right of post and in; third one, over post, under spoke at right of post, over next two and in. Treat eight spokes standing at second end like those at first end, making border with five and weaving with remaining three along second side of basket to first end.

For upper sides, use Double Under-and-Over Weave with two parallel reeds, reversing at posts. Weave to within ½ inch of top of posts.

Border—Beside left post insert well soaked strand of No. 5, 15 inches long, to take place of post in border; wind it once around post, and use it as first spoke. Pass each spoke under spoke at right, over next one, under next two and out, finishing on outside to prevent ends from breaking when wood is put into basket. Twist last spoke at right around post and conceal its end.

Handle—Whittle three rods 46 inches long into points at ends; insert them 1½ inches apart in Triple Weave of sides. Bore holes near their ends and fasten (Figure 18). Weave under and over rods with two flexible No. 3 weavers, bringing gradually together. Fasten them just below border by weaving back and forth through sides, A. Whittle two rods 29 inches long flat along one side; lay these along grooves between rods, B. Wrap all five with double weavers for 1½ inches; lift up two half-rounds and wrap three lower rods 1½ inches. Alternate thus to end of half rounds, curving handle to opposite side. Tie handle down, insert rods in sides and interweave as on first side. Put a tack near top of posts to keep side borders from slipping off. Stain basket or shellac.

Courtesy of Girl Scouts, Rockland County, New York

FIGURE 27—A TENTFUL OF BASKETS MADE FROM MATERIALS GATHERED
BY SCOUTS ON THEIR OWN CAMP GROUNDS

No. 1. Birdhouse of Ash Splints—Covered With Twining of Wisteria
Bark.   Plaited base, 5 inches square, Figure 33.   Twined sides, 7 inches
high, Figure 35.   Simple Splint Border, Figure 36, P. Roof, Figure 73.

No. 2. Sewed Grass Baskets and Mats—Start these with coiling centers,
Figures 46, 47.   Make sides and lids with pine needle stitches, Figure 56.

No. 3. Small Tray For Jewelry; Folding Work Basket—Of braided grasses over splints. Start work basket with Round Splint Base, Figure 34. Weave closely with grass twining to diameter of 8 inches; turn edge over 1 inch; finish with Simple Splint Border, Figure 36, P. Handle, braided raffia or grasses. Weave two similar sections, tie together at back, fasten at front with a loop.

No. 4. Tiny Handled Bag of Rushes—Base, 4 x 1½ inches, Figure 33, D. Sides, plaiting. Openwork border, Figure 60. Handle, rolled rushes, Fig. 61.

No. 5. Covered Jar of Dark Red Cedar Bark Splints—And pale green cat-tail weavers. Round Splint Base, Figure 34, A. Sides, Twining sections with cat-tails, interrupted by Simple Weave with strips of bark, Figure 35, A. Border, Figure 39, G.

No. 6. Round Hanging Basket—Made over a jar with spokes of cedar bark, weaving of cat-tails, and trimming of willow buds. Made like covered jar No. 5, with sides of Simple Weave and braided handle. Tuck willow buds into border. Shellac.

No. 7. Moccasins of Braided Cat-tails—Make braids of split strands. Start an oval braided base for sole, Fig. 56, R. Make one less turn around heel than around toe part. Carry braids over instep in crosses.

No. 8. Hanging Flower Basket—Of dark brown Virginia creeper runners. Simple Base, Fig. 3. Sides, weave in-and-out over nine pairs of spokes to cover a jar. Rapid Braid Border, Fig. 15. Double Braided Handle, Fig. 19, T; fasten with wire.

No. 9. Work Basket of Willow—Sixteen-spoke base, Figure 4, diameter 6 inches. Sides, Simple Weave. Closed Border, No. 1, Figure 12.

No. 10. Large Round Tray—Of willow rods and ash splints. Simple Base, Figure 3, with No. 8 spokes. Weave under-and-over to diameter of 8 inches. Insert extra spokes, weave Wrapping, Figure 35, to diameter of 12 inches. Triple Coil at edge. Sides, 1 inch high. False Braid Border, Figure 36, T.

No. 11. Thermos Holder—Made of ash splints with cat-tail weaving. Round Splint Base, 5 inches in diameter, Figure 34. Insert long splints for sides, weave in-and-out with single cat-tails to top. Simple Splint Border, Figure 36, P. Braided handles.

No. 12. Double Work Basket of Split Willow—Border wrapped with rushes. Round Splint Base, Figure 34, A, using pairs of splints placed flat together. Weave over pairs to diameter of 4 inches. To make center basket, weave upward over upper ones only for 2 inches; handle, a wrapped splint. Use lower splints of pairs for flat base of large basket, diameter, 10 inches; sides Simple Weave, Fig. 35, A, 1 inch lower than small basket.

No. 13. Square Hanging Basket—Of alternate cat-tail and cedar bark weaving. Plaited Base of splints, 5 inches square, Figure 33, A. Sides, Twining with cat-tails, Simple Weave with bark strips, Figure 35, A. Border, Figure 39, G.

No. 14. Tray of Pine Needles—Sewed with raffia split stitches. Oval base 12 x 16 inches, middle section, Fern Stitch, outer section, Wing Stitch, Fig. 56.

CHAPTER XI

WILLOW BASKETS

"And bending osiers into baskets weav'd."—DRYDEN.

ℐN the basket world a distinct place is accorded baskets of willow. Because of its lightness and strength the Romans used willow to make not only baskets and bee-hives, but fences for gardens and vineyards. Pliny writes, "Cato held an osier bed in higher estimation than an olive plantation or than wheat or meadow land." In Europe willow is still the most popular basket material. A United States government bulletin states: "No stock is equal to willow when durable baskets are de-manded."

Willow baskets, however, are not limited in type to sturdy con-tainers such as hampers for dried fruits and nuts, stout shallow trays for bread, and receptacles for eggs. Delicate, beautifully woven willow baskets and mats are widely used; for the rods, of which the weavers are made, are not only slender, but may be split once and then again. To trim their windows, European bakers display their finer products in delicate willow baskets; and finely woven mats of willow are used to keep hot dishes from marring the table.

Nor need one, in considering the utility and variety of willow baskets, forget beauty. The rods have real charm for sensitive eyes and fingers in their texture, slight irregularities and fine satiny smoothness, an added charm in their soft white or pale tan color, while the fineness of the weavers obtained by splitting the rods gives the weaver a sense of working with adaptable and delicate material suitable to beautiful designs, both simple and intricate.

WILLOW GARDENS FOR HOME OR SCHOOL

You may grow willow of your own at home or school, for this plant may be grown in a wide range of soils, from the Arctic Circle to the West Indies, from Norway to Australia. Though it does best in moist soil, this is not essential, as commonly supposed. A willow garden is pretty, while the cutting and peeling of the rods is a simple and delightful operation. Willow rods secured in this way are almost as flexible as the reed you buy, can be used in as many ways, and are far less costly.

The shoots grow rapidly, require little care, and add a touch of beauty uncommon in America, where willow has not had the culti-vation long given it in Europe. The long slender stems and long, slender pale green leaves are as pretty as a hedge for a boundary, and much more practical. The trimming of such a hedge each year would also furnish an abundance of rods for weaving, the shears doing double service for beauty and utility.

The three kinds of willow most successfully grown in America for producing basketry rods are the American green willow, (*Salix amygdalina L*); the purple, or Welsh, willow *(Salix purpurea L)*; and the Caspian, or Lemley, willow, *(Salix pentandra, major and minor)*.

HOW TO PLANT

Plant the cuttings as soon as frost is out of the ground early in spring while the ground is moist and the air cool. If the buds are opening, put the rods in buckets of water and cover with wet sacks to protect them from sun and air. If the soil is soft the cuttings may be set in holes made with dibble—a stick or an iron bar 3 feet long and ⅜ to ⅝ inches in diameter, sharpened at one end to a stubby point so the cutting will go to the bottom of the hole. Fasten a handle or cross piece to the top of the stick for convenience. Push the stick in the ground just far enough to make room for the cutting which should be inserted with about 2 inches above ground, and at least one bud showing.

The number and length of rods that will develop will depend largely upon the spacing of the cuttings. If the soil is rich, space the cuttings 6 inches apart and the rows 18 inches; if medium, space them 6 x 24 inches, (purple willow, 12 x 24); and if poor, space them 9 x 24 inches, (purple willow, 12 x 36). For full information see Farmer's Bulletin, No. 622, Basket Willow Culture, United States Department of Agriculture.

HARVESTING WILLOW RODS

The rods are cut close to the main stem. From the stub thus left many healthy young shoots will develop. These are allowed to grow until the following fall or spring and then harvested. Cut with sharp pruning shears.

Various ways of handling the rods after cutting produce three kinds: 1. white, with the bark peeled off; 2. tan, with the bark peeled off; 3. brown or unpeeled.

1. White Rods—Cut the willows in early spring just after the sap begins to rise and the buds to swell, lay them in wet soil with some old willow peelings and let them ferment in the heat for several weeks. When the bark loosens strip it from the rods, wash the white rods clean and dry them in the sun to keep them from molding. Before using, soak them in tepid water for an hour, then wrap them in a damp cloth to soften or mellow still more.

2. *Tan or Buffed Rods*—Cut the shoots in the fall after the leaves have gone or in the spring before the sap begins to rise, and boil them in water with the bark left on, from four to six hours. The tanin in the bark gives them their tan color and the process of boiling is called "buffing." When cool, peel the bark off and dry the rods in the sun and air. Before using, soak in tepid water for an hour and wrap in a damp cloth to mellow. These buffed rods make our familiar golden brown picnic hampers, clothes baskets, shopping and fishing baskets, being of a color that does not readily show soil.

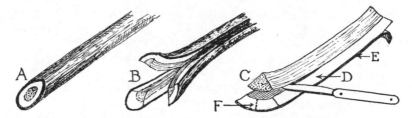

FIGURE 28—SPLITTING A WILLOW ROD INTO THREE STRIPS

3. *Brown or Unpeeled Rods*—Are used for woodsy-looking baskets, flower baskets, rustic furniture and coarse willow work. Gather the rods in late autumn after the leaves have fallen, or in early spring before the sap begins to rise, and dry them in the wind and sun to keep them from molding. Before using, soak them in water for two or three days and wrap them in a damp towel for a day more to mellow.

WILLOW BUDS

The pale gray-green willow buds with graceful tapering points that form during the summer, may be gathered in the fall, dried and used in clusters to ornament baskets. Single buds may be woven into the border. Two or three are effective when used in a group at the sides of a handle, or over the arch. When these buds are shellaced they retain their color and are lovely with baskets of cedar bark, green cat-tails or unpeeled vines.

[58]

HINTS FOR USING WILLOW

After soaking always wrap rods in a damp towel to mellow.

The base is thicker than the tip of a willow rod. Therefore, in piecing, if rod-weaver ends with butt end, begin new weaver with butt end; if it ends with tip, begin new end with tip.

When inserting side spokes, trim rods with a single long diagonal cut at their thick ends, making a sharp point to slip into weaving easily.

In bending willow spokes up for the sides of a basket, make a slight dent at their turning point, on the inside of the rod, by pricking them with an awl, or using pincers.

Learn to split willow into fine strips for starting baskets and for weaving fine ones, Figure 28.

SPLITTING WILLOW RODS INTO STRIPS FOR FINE WEAVING—FIGURE 28 AND FIGURE 2

The best method of splitting willow rods is that still used by the Indian. Soak the rods well and cut them diagonally across one end, as at A. With a finger nail or the teeth divide this end into three triangular segments, splitting from the center out, as at B. Hold the lower segment tightly between the teeth, and take each of the other two segments between the thumb and forefinger of each hand. This position is shown by the girl at left foreground of frontispiece. Pull slowly downward and outward with both hands until there is an even tension between all three segments, then quickly move both hands downward, dividing the rod into three parts. The splitting is done rapidly after the initial division of the end of the rod is made. Each segment has a brittle woody layer on the inside of the inner bark, shown at C. Scrape this away with the finger nail or a knife, and use the flexible strip of white inner bark, D, with or without the dark outer bark, E, for weaving. The Indian obtains still finer strips by splitting each of the three segments in half, as shown by dotted line at F, thus obtaining six minute strips from a single rod.

[59]

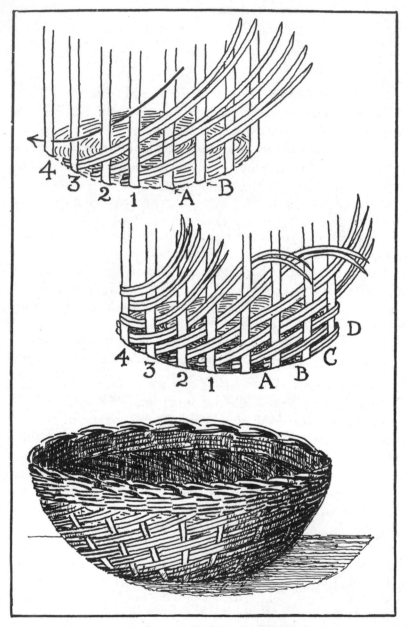

FIGURE 29—WORK BASKET USING "SLEWING" WEAVE

"SLEWING," A USEFUL WILLOW WEAVE—Figure 29

A pretty texture is given light willow baskets by weaving pairs of short willow rods upward in a diagonal direction. This weave, called "slewing," is as useful as it is effective, conveniently employing short willow withes, or cut pieces of any material.

Slewing is used mostly for the sides of a basket. Count side spokes and select twice as many rods as this number for weaving, all having about same length and thickness. Arrange in pairs and insert a pair behind any spoke, as at Figure 29, spoke No. 1. Carry this pair in front of next spoke at right, A, and behind second spoke at right, B. Insert pairs of rods in succession behind each spoke at left of No. 1, at Nos. 2, 3, 4, etc., and carry each pair to right, over a spoke and under a spoke, making one complete stroke. Continue above first round, taking each pair next at left in succession, and carrying it toward right for a complete stroke. In last or top round, leave tips of each pair behind spoke of their last stroke. Before making border, bring basket up into shape by adding several rows of Pairing or Triple Weave. This top section of solid weaving is shown in the drawing, a fine finish to the beautiful diagonal texture of the basket surface below.

WILLOW WEAVE WITH ONE WEAVER

As willow withes do not come in long pieces, weaving with them entails frequent piecing. The following weave has been thought out by English weavers to make a rhythmic succession of tapering withes, each one used only once around the basket. Start with an odd number of spokes. After turning these up for sides, select willow rods long enough to go once around basket with a few inches to spare. Insert a rod with its thick end behind a spoke, and weave once around basket with in-and-out weaving, finishing tip of weaver behind same spoke. Insert thick end of next weaver behind spoke just at left of first spoke, and weave it once around. Continue using a new rod for each row, inserting its butt one spoke to left of starting spoke of preceding weaver, and finishing its tip behind same spoke. Before weaving border, put in a round or more of Pairing or Triple Weave to secure shape of basket. The butt ends lying next to tapering ends in successive rows form a texture contrast which shows in an attractive spiral curve around basket.

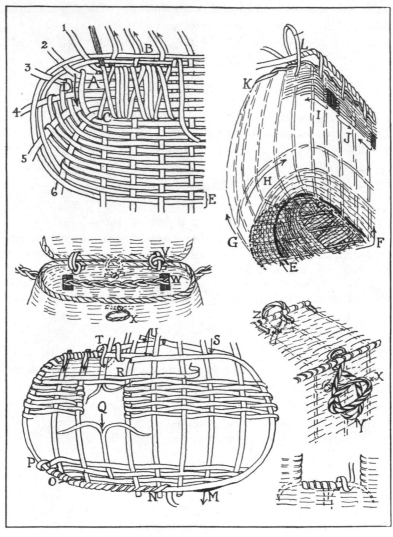

FIGURE 30—DIAGRAMS OF A STURDY REED FISHING BASKET
PHOTOGRAPH, FIGURE 12-A

FISHING BASKET OF WILLOW OR REED—Figure 30 and Figure 12-A

This strong fishing basket is conveniently shaped, with openings at back for shoulder strap and an opening in lid to drop fish through.

Materials—Spokes, size No. 5. Weavers, No. 3. Rim of lid, No. 8. Wrapping, No. 2 or narrow cane.

Base—The core of base, A, lies close to basket back, B. Place six long spokes of No. 5, 36 inches long, across nine short spokes, 28 inches long. Wrap with cane or No. 2 reed, as at C. Use ends of long spoke No. 1 for corners; insert extra spoke, shaded, to make uneven number. Weave back and forth across front only, as at D, reversing at Nos. 2, 3, 4, 5 and 6 in order. Weave all around with one weaver, as at shaded row, E; bend back spokes, F, vertical to make weaving of sides, H, slope upward.

Sides and Border—When flat base, shaded, measures 12 x 6 inches, bend front spokes, G, upward and weave in shape shown until back is 6 inches high. Make openings, I, by reversing weaving toward front at spokes next to corners; also weave between holes at back, J. When holes are 1 inch deep, weave around basket for 1 inch, oval at top measuring 10 x 5 inches. Use Closed Border No. 2, at K; or finish with row of Pairing, trim spokes close, and stitch round rod, L, above edge, wrapping it between fastenings.

Lid—Bend a No. 8 rod, 30 inches long, to shape of basket top; tie ends together. Split front of rod and insert No. 5 spokes at 1-inch intervals, as at M. Wrap with fine reed or cane, as at N, and weave back and forth across lid with same strand, as at O, with extra wrappings at sides to make a close edge, as at P. Weave in-and-out for 3 inches. Clip spokes flush with front edge. To make opening, split a spoke, as at Q; conceal its ends in weaving; reverse weaving at left and right taking extra wrappings around edges. When hole is 2 inches square, weave 1 inch above it, as at R, inserting a new spoke and concealing its split ends. Wrap top and bottom edges of opening, as at lower right of Figure 30. Split rod at back of lid, as at S, and insert spokes through slit. Bind two halves together, as at T, stitching down at intervals into woven part of lid, through holes in spokes made with an awl. Splice ends together, as at U.

Fasten lid to basket with knotted strand, V. Insert strap through holes, W. To close lid, attach a twisted ring of No. 3 reed, 2 inches below top front, as at X, inserting both ends through same hole and tying them with knot inside basket. This ring turns around over twisted loop, Y, fastened to center front of lid. A loop may be made at top back of basket to hang it by, as at Z (see Figure 20).

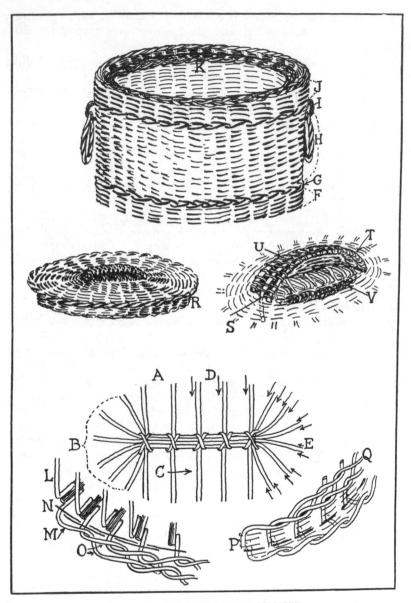

Figure 31—WILLOW PICNIC HAMPER

WILLOW PICNIC HAMPER—Figure 31

This convenient hamper for picnics or for carrying small articles in cars has a spacious oval shape and a lid that fits well down into the basket.

Materials—Spokes, size No. 10 for base, No. 5 for sides. Weavers, Nos. 3 and 4.

Base—Make oval with five spokes, A, of No. 10, 9 inches long, and six spokes, B, 12 inches long. Weave in-and-out with two strands of No. 3 for 2 inches, as far as C; change to No. 4 and weave until oval measures 9 x 12 inches.

Sides—Insert thirty-four No. 5 spokes, 20 inches long, one at each side spoke, D, arrows, and two each at six end spokes, E. Finish base edge with Four-rod Coil using No. 4; bend spokes up and continue Four-rod Weaving for four rows, F. Finish section F with Reverse Four-rod Coil making arrow, G, (Figure 9). Weave section H, 5 inches high, with Triple Weave and No. 4 weavers. Make Arrow at I like G, and Four-rod Weaving, J, like F. (Section F may be Triple Weave finishing with Three-rod Arrow, with Pairing Weave for sides, H.)

Border—Pass each spoke in succession under two spokes at right and over following three, bringing them out on inside of basket. Weave flat shelf around them with Pairing using No. 3, ending spokes with two successive Finishing Twists, (Figure 17). See K above.

Lid—Outer rim, R, fits down on shelf just made, and vertical collar slips down within basket. Start lid like base with five spokes, A, 8 inches long, and six spokes, B, 11 inches long. At C use Triple Weave until lid measures 10½ x 7½ inches. For outer rim and collar insert forty-four spokes of No. 4, 12 inches long, one at each side of spokes, as at L and M. Turn lid over. Bend left spokes upward, as at L; carry right ones out to make border, as at M. Weave one row Pairing or Simple Weave, N, over border spokes, and finish with two successive Finishing Twists, M and O. Outside measurement of border is 8¾ x 11¾ inches, fitting within basket border measuring 9 x 12 inches on inside. Weave six vertical rows around L-spokes with No. 3, as at P; end spokes with two Finishing Twists, Q.

Handle—A half-circle is made of three parallel rods covered with in-and-out weaving. Insert strand, S, of No. 4, 36 inches long, at one end of central core, with 2-inch end under lid. Curve rod 1 inch above lid, as at U, and insert at other end, T; bring it back under lid, and out at left of S. Curve upward at left of first curve and insert again at left of T; bring end back under lid again and out at right of first curve. Curve upward at right of U, and insert at right of T. Weave closely in and out of three curves with fine well soaked weaver fastened under lid. Fasten all ends together under lid with raffia, as at V. Add ring handles to sides of basket, (Figure 20).

[65]

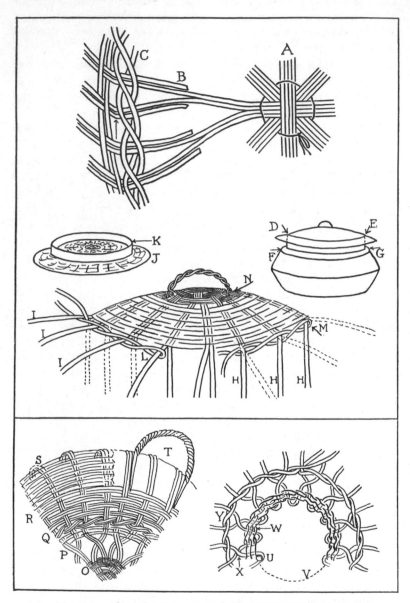

FIGURE 32-A—*Above*, DIAGRAMS OF EVER-READY WORK BASKET.
Below, COVERING A PLATE WITH VINE, WILLOW OR REED

EVER-READY WORK BASKET—Figures 32, 32-A

This work basket is made with a special compartment in its lid for a pin cushion, see photo on next page. When the basket is opened one discovers the cushion under the lid, with pins, needles and scissors all ready for service.

Materials—Spokes of vine, willow or reed, size No. 4. Weavers, No. 3. Several strands No. 2.

Base—Group sixteen spokes 32 inches long in fours, cross at their centers; fasten with cord, as at A. Start a Sixteen-spoke Base, (Figure 4) with No. 2. Change to No. 3, add a second weaver; weave alternately until base is 7 or 8 inches wide. Insert thirty-two 8-inch spokes, one beside each base spoke, as at B. Separate spokes into pairs at edge of base with Triple Weave, C.

Sides—Soak basket, pinch spokes, bend upward. Weave in and out for 2 inches with No. 3, sloping sides at 45 degrees, to middle of basket, widest part. At this point weave Triple Coil over the pairs, with No. 4, (Figure 9). Above coil use Simple Weave for 1½ inches, drawing spokes in to a diameter of 7 or 8 inches at top, and finishing with four rows of Triple with No. 3. Clip off inserted spokes, leaving single ones for border.

Border—Carry each spoke behind two spokes at its right, in front of third and fourth and behind fifth. Secure ends with Finishing Twist, (Figure 12).

Cover—Weave cover like base with sixteen 30-inch spokes, gradually bending spokes to a dome shape until diameter at edge, D to E, is ½ inch less than diameter of top of basket, F to G. For upper ledge of cover, J, carry left spoke of each pair out horizontally, as at I; for collar, K, bend each right spoke down vertically, as at H. Weave ledge first, tying H spokes together with string. Use looped No. 3 weaver to start Pairing over I spokes, as at L, and weave until ledge comes out above widest part of basket. For border, carry each spoke over first spoke at its right, under second spoke, over third and behind fourth. The Finishing Twist may be added.

To make vertical collar, K, to slip into top of basket, turn lid upside down. Start pairing over H spokes with a looped No. 3 weaver, M, and weave straight for ¾ inch. For border, pass each end, now on inside, over first end at its right and behind second— Finishing Twist used twice. Make saw-dust pin-cushion, cover with cretonne, fasten inside lid. Sew band near edge to hold scissors. If preferred, leave lid unfilled to hold equipment while sewing, omitting basket handle so lid will lie flat on table.

Handle—Make twisted handle (Figure 18) with No. 3 strand 10 inches long, looped over a group of spokes, as at N, and measuring 2 inches across.

FIGURE 32—EVER-READY WORK BASKET

COVERING A PLATE WITH VINE, WILLOW, OR REED
—FIGURE 32-A

An attractive sandwich tray is made by weaving closely over the bottom of a plate or piece of pottery, with fine basketry materials. This woven cover protects the plate, and if handles are added makes it more convenient than a plain plate. Two methods of weaving the cover are shown, Figure 32-A, below. In diagram at left, entire bottom of plate is covered; in that at right weaving begins at raised bottom ring of plate, on which it rests.

First Method—Start a Sixteen-spoke Base (Figure 4) as at O, using No. 2 spokes and two fine weavers, No. 0 or 1. Follow this with open-work section, P; a row of Double Pairing, Q, (Figure 8); and a section of Double or Simple Weave, R, (Figure 7). Bend spokes down over edge of plate, as at S; weave several rows on the inside close to edge. Finish with Closed Border No. 2 (Figure 12). Insert two handle rods, size No. 6 or 7, their ends whittled to points, opposite each other in the border; wrap over them with a fine strand, as at T, tying both ends securely in weaving.

Second Method—There is no regular base; the weaving is started around bottom ring of plate, over spokes bent double. A good plan is to start weaving on a board, thumb-tacking folded spokes down at their loops as at U. On a smooth board draw a circle the size of plate ring, dotted line, V. Cut twelve spokes of fine reed, soak until pliable, bend double and thumb-tack the loops around circle, U. Start Pairing over both ends of loops, making several rows around circle, W. Cross spokes, X; put in another round of Pairing, Y. Remove woven start from board, turn plate upside down, lay weaving over bottom of plate. Continue Pairing or Simple Weave, pulling spokes snugly around plate to cover part that rises upward. Bend spokes down over edge; finish with Closed Border No. 2.

PART II—FLAT BASKETRY MATERIALS

CHAPTER XII

WEAVING WITH FLAT BASKETRY MATERIALS

ATURE's skillful artistry in weathering her barks and tinting the inner wood to many wonderful tones—a transformation gently wrought through the changing seasons—has made ready for our use quantities of soft-hued barks and roots that may be split into flat weavers. The various textures of the materials seem to inspire their own characteristic basket forms. Frequently their flatness and flexibility make them excellent for plaiting, a weave in which even strands interlace to form a mat-like surface, (Figure 33). Again flat strips may form the warp of a basket, its foundation of spokes, with a weft of narrower flat weavers or pliable materials,—soft stems, leaves, grasses. These are woven over the flat splints in many ways, with rows of weaving close together or with spaces left between, (Figure 35). Some soft weaving materials, like long leathery rushes or cane stems are crushed flat and used for plaiting. These too are dyed by the sun and rain almost every pastel shade, so that baskets woven of them are exceptionally lovely.

In describing the ways in which flat basketry materials are used, let us see first how they are put together to form basket bases; secondly, how they are woven into various stitches to form the sides of baskets; and lastly, how they are made into borders for the tops of baskets.

1. BASES OF FLAT MATERIALS
FIGURES 33 AND 34

Bases woven with flat materials are either of straight outline, like square or oblong bases, or of curved outline, like round or oval bases.

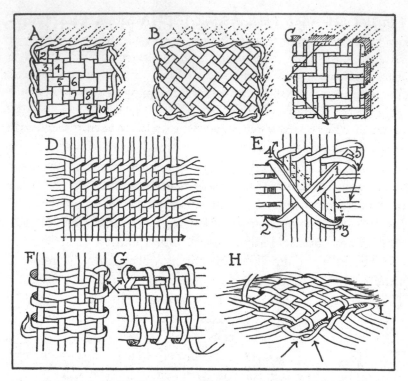

FIGURE 33—FLAT STRAND BASES WITH STRAIGHT OUTLINES
A—Plaited base with checked weave. B—Plaited base with diagonal checks.
C—Plaited base with twilled stitches. D—Twined base. E—Cross-tie center.
F, G, H—Base with double center

FLAT STRAND BASES OF STRAIGHT OUTLINE—
FIGURE 33

Plaited Base With Checked Weave, A—Attractive for trays.
Interlace two sets of splints the same width at right angles to each
other in single checks. First lay down splint 1, upper left; cross
it with opposite splint 2; interlace splints according to number,
first a horizontal, then a vertical. Hold ends down with spraddle
tacks; finish edge with Pairing Weave. To make oblong checked
base, use more splints along one side than along side at right angles
to it.

Plaited Base With Diagonal Checks, B—Make this base similar
to that at A, but interlace splints diagonally. Tack splints down
on block of wood desired size to secure them; turn them up over
edges of block for sides.

Plaited Base With Twilled Stitches, C—A pattern base. Interlace two sets of splints at right angles to each other in a twilled pattern. Cross each splint under and over several splints at a time instead of just one as in checked plaiting, and in successive rows take each stitch one splint farther to left or right of stitch in preceding row, to shift twilling diagonally. Twilled bases may be square or oblong; the stitches may be parallel or turned diagonally to sides, as shown by arrows at C.

Twined Base, D—Good for light pack baskets. Twine across a set of parallel splints with a second set of splints in pairs. First lay several single spokes parallel on a table, shown vertically; hold them down with a heavy board as at arrow. Weave across them at right angles with Pairing Weave, with two new weavers for each row. To form basket sides, keep twining weavers in pairs and use as pairs of spokes; to make sides flare outward, separate pairs into single spokes.

Cross-tie Center, E—Easy to make and strong. Lay set of three or four parallel splints at right angles to second set of same number. Place two narrow flat weavers together; start their ends at upper right corner of splints, 1. Carry them diagonally across splints to lower left corner, up under lower splints, 2; down across other two corners, 3; and up under all splints from lower right to upper left corner, dotted lines, 4. At this corner start twining with both ends around splints, binding starting ends in weaving, 5. To keep this center square, pull weavers out slightly at each corner; otherwise it tends to be circular.

Base With Double Center, F, G, H—Very strong; woven in two sections. Weave start at F with single strand interlacing vertical splints; weave start at G with strand interlacing same number of horizontal splints; fasten ends as at arrows. Lay F on top of G with splints at right angles, H. Weave in-and-out with one weaver until it reaches other weaver at corner, I; then twine around all splints with both weavers. Pull first round up taut, forcing two layers into curve; continue with same tension until curve is secure; weave normally for rest of base, inserting extra splints at four corners, arrows, to fill in spaces. Make curve concave for stationary baskets, convex for hanging baskets and water bottles.

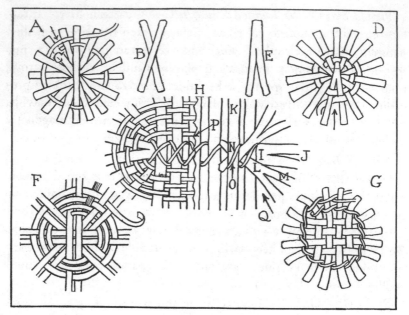

FIGURE 34—FLAT STRAND BASES WITH CURVED OUTLINES
A-C—Round splint base with even number of spokes. D—Round splint base with
uneven number of spokes. F—Base with spokes in pairs. G—Plaited center within
twining. H—Oval splint base

FLAT STRAND BASES OF CURVED OUTLINE—FIGURE 34

Round Splint Base With Even Number of Spokes, A—A strong
thick base. Select smooth splints, cut eight strips ½ inch wide or
wider for spokes, and others ⅛ to ¼ inch wide for weavers. Lay
spokes together as at B, each one above the last, centers crossing.
Start weaving under and over the splints, as at C. After first
round, skip a spoke in each round, passing over two spokes in a
single stitch, as at arrow, just above skipping of preceding row.
Weave in-an-out with one weaver until base measures desired
diameter. Insert other splints for sides.

Round Splint Base With Uneven Number of Spokes, D—This
start is like that just described except that one spoke-end is split
in two, making an uneven number of ends for a single strand to
weave around. Cut six spokes of even width and a seventh with
one end double this width. Split this in two parts, as at E, giving
an uneven number of spoke-ends to weave over. Start base like
that at A, and weave under-and-over spokes in successive rounds
with a single weaver without skipping.

Round Splint Base With Spokes in Pairs, F—Moderately strong. Group eight spokes in pairs; cross them first vertically and horizontally then diagonally. Weave twice around pairs with a fine weaver, passing over straight groups and under diagonal ones; then separate pairs into single spokes, add extra spoke, shaded, to make uneven number, and continue weaving in-and-out with a single weaver. For base of coarse texture, add an extra pair of spokes instead of a single one and continue weaving in-and-out of odd number of pairs.

Plaited Center Within Twining, G—Excellent for bread baskets and desk trays; not very strong; made in any size. Interweave two sets splints at right angles to each other, and encircle plaited center with rows of Twining. First follow directions for Plaited Base, Figure 33, A. Then fold weaver double and start twining around center in successive rounds. To make base oval or oblong, use more splints along one side than along side at right angles to it.

Oval Splint Base, H—Similar to oval bases made with round rods in Figure 5. Cut a long wide splint, I, for center; split in two pieces at each end, J. Lay several short splints, K, across it. To fill in corners, insert shaped splints, L, cut wide at outer end which is split into two parts, M, and narrow at inner end which is inserted under cross splints at N. Wrap splints at their intersections with fine strand, O, wrapping first to right, then reversing to left to form crosses over first wrappings. Weave in-and-out with single weaver, as at P, adding odd end at Q to make uneven number. Use Pairing Weave around base edge.

BASKET COVERS MADE OF FLAT MATERIALS

Start any cover—round, square or oval—like its corresponding base in Figures 33 and 34. For a lid with turned over edges, weave flat surface a trifle wider than top of basket, soak splints and turn them down over top edge of basket; weave several rows and fasten them to a border splint, Figure 36, P. For a flat square lid without turned over edges, weave a surface like section F in Figure 33; take extra turns at sides to fill in gaps; finish spokes with a border, inserting spokes on empty sides. For a flat round lid, weave a disc like Figure 34, A, lay a narrow splint around edge; bind with over and over stitches.

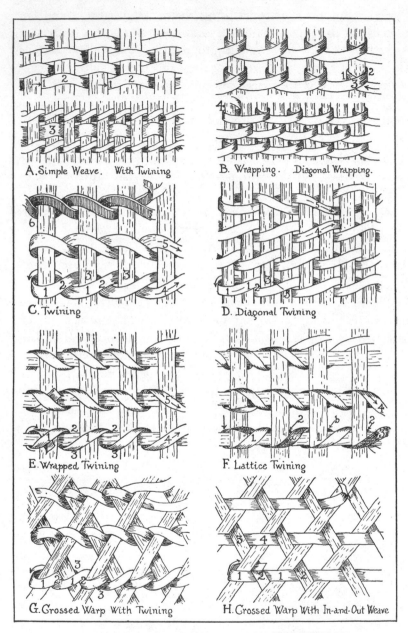

A. Simple Weave. With Twining
B. Wrapping. Diagonal Wrapping.
C. Twining
D. Diagonal Twining
E. Wrapped Twining
F. Lattice Twining
G. Crossed Warp With Twining
H. Crossed Warp With In-and-Out Weave

FIGURE 35—WEAVING STITCHES OF FLAT MATERIALS

2. WEAVING STITCHES OF FLAT MATERIALS—
FIGURES 33, 35

Plaiting, Figure 33, A—For sides of a plaited basket, bend spokes upward, split one of them in two at base of sides, and weave in and out with single strand same width as splint-spokes. (Plaited bases, Figure 33.)

Twilling, Figure 33, C—For sides of a twilled basket, bend spokes upward, split one of them in two to give uneven number and continue same pattern as base, weaving under and over two or more spokes with single weaver same width as spokes.

Simple Weave, Figure 35, A—Weave continuously under a spoke, A, 1, over the next, A, 2, and under-and-over successive spokes all around basket. If number of spokes is uneven, use one weaver; if even, use two. A row of Simple Weave may be inserted between sections of Twining, as at A, 3.

Wrapping, B—Wrap a flexible weaver around more rigid warp spokes. Loop weaver over its own end, B, arrow, pass it in front of next spoke, 1, around, back of it, 2, out to front again over wrapping, 3, then to next spoke. Rows may be close together or with spaces between.

Diagonal Wrapping, B, 4—Wrap spokes as for regular wrapping but skip spoke between wrappings. Number of spokes must be uneven to make diagonal texture.

Twining or Pairing, C—Fold weaver double and loop it around a spoke, C, arrow. Carry each weaving end in turn in front of first spoke at right, C, 1; twist it over other weaver, 2; and carry it back of next spoke, 3. For upward twining twist lower weaver over upper one, 4; for downward twining, twist upper weaver over lower one, 5. Two oppositely twisted rows pushed close together form a Twining Arrow.

Three-strand Twining—Called Triple Weave in Part I, Figure 9. May be executed over flat foundation splints, as over round spokes.

Overlay Twining, C, 6—Twining strands may be overlaid with grass strips C, 6. Carry these along on face of weavers. To make basket pattern, use colored overlay strands wherever motif occurs; cut them out where background only is to show.

Diagonal Twining, D—Start with uneven number of spokes. Fold strand double; loop it around a spoke, D, arrow. Carry each end in turn in front of two spokes at right, 1-1, over other weaver, 2, and back of next two spokes, 3-3. Two rows twisted in opposite direction, 4 and 5, make a Twining Arrow.

Wrapped Twining, E—Twine with one weaver at crossing of horizontal and vertical rods. Fasten weaver at E, arrow, carry it up over first crossing, 1, down back of horizontal rod, 2, and out from under rod ready for next crossing of weaver, 3. Twine upward, 4, or downward, 5.

Lattice Twining, F—Twine with two weavers at crossings of vertical and horizontal rods. Fold weaver double; loop it back of horizontal rod, F, arrow. Carry each weaver in turn up over next crossing, 1, and down, back of next crossing to it, 2. Second weaver, a-b, is shaded. Twine upward, 3, or downward, 4.

Crossed Warp with Twining, G—Cross spokes diagonally. Fold weaver double; loop it below crossing, G, arrow. Twine each end in turn over spoke at its right, 1, over other weaver, 2, and back of next spoke slanting in opposite direction, 3.

Crossed Warp With In-and-Out Weaving, H—Cross spokes diagonally. Fasten weaving end, H, arrow. Pass weaver over upper spoke of crossing, 1, back of lower spoke, 2, over next one, 1, etc., weaving under and over spokes below successive crossings. Always pass weaver under lower spoke, 3, and over upper one, 4.

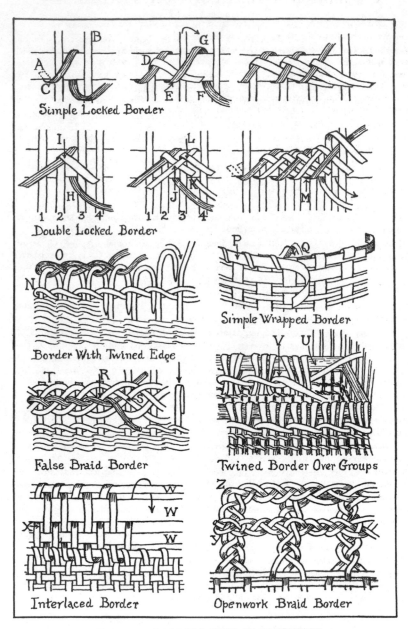

Simple Locked Border

Double Locked Border

Border With Twined Edge

Simple Wrapped Border

False Braid Border

Twined Border Over Groups

Interlaced Border

Openwork Braid Border

FIGURE 36—BORDERS OF FLAT MATERIALS

[76]

3. BORDERS OF FLAT MATERIALS—Figure 36

Flat spokes in borders may be finished in many useful and beautiful ways. Some of them are adaptable to round weaving materials.

Simple Locked Splint Border, A-G—Strong, simple finish. Lay a splint, A, back of basket spokes, B. Wrap flexible strand, C, upward to right, over first spoke, in between first two standing spokes, down, back of splint and out; turn left spoke, D, down over it. Repeat as follows: * Wrap winding strand upward to right over turned down spoke, (E) in between next two standing spokes, down, back of splint, and out between same spokes, (F); turn left standing spoke down over it, (G). Repeat from *.

Double Locked Splint Border, H-M—Two winding strands are used instead of one. Pass left one, shaded, up to right across two spokes, Nos. 1 and 2; in between standing spokes Nos. 2 and 3, down, back of splint and out between same spokes, H. Turn left spoke, No. 2, down over it, I, arrow. Cross second winding strand, unshaded, over turned down spoke No. 2, as at J, in front of next spoke, No. 3, in between next two standing spokes, Nos. 3 and 4, down, back of splint and out between same spokes, K. Turn left spoke, L, over it. Repeat as follows: * Wind each strand in succession, always taking left one, up to right, over spokes already turned down, in between next two standing spokes, down, back of wide splint and out between same two standing spokes. Turn left spoke down over it. Repeat from *.

Open Border With Twined Edge, N-O—For flexible spokes. Finish basket with row of Twining, N. Turn spokes over in loops (Figure 11). Run a row of Twining along tops of loops.

Simple Wrapped Splint Border, P-Q. Narrow, flat edge. Turn splints down over last row,—those inside, out; those outside, in. Lay flat splint, P, around outside of row, and second splint, shaded, around inside. Bind these to last row with narrow wrapping strand, Q.

False Braid Border With Twining, R-T—For stiff spokes. Start separate four-strand braid with two weavers folded double. As each two strands cross at center of braid, bring them in front of spoke, S, and attach to spoke with a twist of the strands, R. Trim spokes off level with braid, T. If spokes are flexible, bend over as at arrow before attaching braid.

Twined Border Over Groups of Spokes, U-V—For large number of spokes. Lay wide splint around inside top of basket, U. Turn spokes over this to inside in groups; fasten them to same spokes with two twining weavers, V. For rustic basket, lay splint on outside, turn spokes over from inside; trim to 1-inch fringe.

Interlaced Border, W-X—Adds height to basket. Place several splints, W, parallel to top of basket. Interweave fairly stiff weaver, X, vertically in-and-out of splints and around top row of basket.

Openwork Braid Border, Y-Z—Braid spokes upward above last row, using six spokes in double braid if spokes are close. Start separate braid, Y, around spoke-braid, braid horizontally all around basket, passing around each vertical braid. Start top braid, Z, as continuation of a spoke-braid and ½ to 1 inch above first braid. Gather strands of each braid into it in passing; drop shorter strands to keep braid even; fasten the last ends in through braid at starting point, Z.

Border with Overlapping Spokes, Figure 39, G-K—The splint spokes of a border may overlap to form a rhythmic succession of folds, as in the border of the kindling basket, Figure 39.

Courtesy of Gene Weltfish

FIGURE 37—A YOUNG SQUAW AND AN OLD SQUAW MAKING BURDEN
BASKETS

Left—Wicker-work basket; under and over weave. Girl from the 3rd Hopi Mesa,
Arizona, finishing the top of a rabbitbush basket by breaking off extra spokes before
weaving borders. *Right*—Twined basket, pairing weave. Woman from Mescalero, New
Mexico, making a twined stitch with one strand of yucca and another of sumach

In various basket forms, the Indian squaw, pondering deeply the
Nature she knew and loved, wove amazing serviceability and
beauty. Her motifs from Nature, conventionalized indeed because of the limited plasticity of her media, identify her in the
tribal emblems depicted and tell us of her joy and pride in her
craft. Sitting on a plaited mat before her wigwam, contentedly
she wove, in the warm rays of the sun, a basket of wiry grasses to
hold grains of wheat or maize, or to gather berries or nuts from
the neighboring fields; and as the basket neared completion, there
grew beneath her devoted fingers some tribal or religious design,—
symbols of rain clouds or of sun, the eagle's flight, or the zig-zag
motion of creeping things. She stopped the rhythmic motion of
her fingers and set aside her work to go for water to the murmur-
ing creek, a basket-covered jug under her arm; and, refreshed,
scouted high over the ledges or low in the brushwood for roots and
berries—the sources of her richly colored dyes. Nimble-footed,
she returned and entered the wigwam—a wicker framework of
twigs.

CHAPTER XIII

SPLIT-ROOT BASKETS

"And each one had a little wicker basket,
Made of fine twigs entraylèd curiously,
In which they gathered flowers to fill their flasket."
—EDMUND SPENSER

ERHAPS you've seen an uprooted tree, and tried to break one of the long, thin, fibrous root-tendrils, to find it unexpectedly, almost unbelievably strong and pliable, practically unbreakable. When the American Indians wanted particularly durable baskets, they pressed such roots into their service: alder, willow, yellow pine, black hemlock, yucca, locust, to mention only a few.

The process of preparing the roots for use, as practised by the Indian, is fairly simple. With a root-digger or a hooked knife, the squaw cuts long sections about the size of her finger from roots, especially roots of cedar and spruce, and buries them in the ground to keep moist until needed. Then, after scraping with a sharp stone, shell, or knife, she hangs them up for partial drying, away from the sun. The careful splitting comes next. This process is effected by running an awl through the lengths of root. Sometimes the roots are steamed or boiled; for they split most easily when damp and warm. The sugar pine, in particular, is steamed by burying in damp sand under a fire, while the Digger pine is warmed in hot damp ashes and split before it cools. The roots of the Sitka pine are usually boiled. It would not be difficult to steam one's roots by any of these methods. When split, the thinnest, evenest strips of the roots are used for sewing or weaving, while the imperfect ones are put into bundles for coiling foundations. Usually slender unsplit rootlets are used for spokes, the split roots for weavers.

Length and toughness are, however, not the only valued characteristics of roots; they are attractively colored—black, rich brown, red, maroon, according to the kind of tree or shrub and, perhaps, also to the mineral content of the soil. The Indians have long known, certainly, of the color values in the soil, for they use it as a natural dyeing vat, burying in it bark and split stems whose pale color they wish to darken for their design. Several days underground, in soil that contains iron, will give to stems a dark brown tone; a week or longer, a black color.

FIGURE 38—OPENWORK CARRYING BASKET WITH BURDEN STRAP

OPENWORK CARRYING BASKET WITH BURDEN STRAP
—FIGURE 38

Lightness is suggested by the very design and texture of this openwork basket to be slung over the shoulder by its convenient flat strap handle. Its spokes of split roots are delicately interspersed here and there with overlaid strands of lustrous white grasses to add life to the texture. The weaving, too, is executed in stripes with wide bands of tan pairing followed by narrower sections of dark brown or red weavers.

Materials—Spokes, split roots ¼ inch wide. Weavers, fine split roots or strips of tough bark.

Base and Sides—Basket measures 10 inches high, and 10 inches wide at open border. Make a twined base like that shown in Figure 33, D, the pairs of split spruce root weavers holding parallel splints together. Use both spokes and weavers of base as side spokes and start base of sides with several rows of pairing, using dark brown bark weavers. Follow this section with five rows of pairing with lighter bark weavers. Then alternate with three rows of dark and five rows of light to top, with spaces of ¼ inch or more between all rows of pairing. Finish with three rows of dark. Above this make white band shown in photograph with two rows of Simple Weave using white cane or grasses. Strips of white among spokes are made by laying fibers of grass or straw over some of the split root spokes.

Border—Follow diagram and directions for Openwork Braid Border, Figure 36, Z. Use six spokes for each vertical braid, two spokes for each strand, and make entire border about 2 inches wide.

Handle—See diagram in Figure 60. This flat braided handle lies comfortably over shoulders, around neck or across chest. Begin handle by tying several long fibrous strands around border of basket, Figure 60, A. Braid with these in three-strand braid for 5 or 6 inches up to arrow, gradually adding more grasses. At this point separate strands into groups to make a six- or eight-strand braid, and plait them in and out over to opposite arrow. Here narrow braid to three strands and braid down to rim of basket at B, tying knot around border with remaining grasses.

CHAPTER XIV

BASKETS OF BARK

*"A toss of my cap to the cedars,
The loveliest things that be."*

ASKETS made from the inner bark of trees like cedar, red-bud or birch, are of lovely soft wood tones—ivory, brown, red—always strong, beautiful and useful. The part of the bark split for weaving is the light inner bark, separated from the dark outer bark by the tree's active region of growth—the moist cambium layer. Here the tree puts on each year a layer or ring of growth. This new wood is easily split into weaving strips. A fallen log or a broken branch will furnish a quantity of material. Soak the log several weeks in a pool, remove the outer bark, then peel the layers off in strips by running a knife beneath them. They may be cut any width and their texture made smooth by scraping with a sharp edge or rubbing with sandpaper.

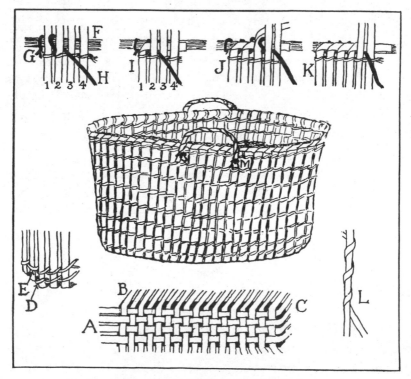

FIGURE 39—CEDAR BARK KINDLING BASKET

The cinnamon-colored inner bark of the red cedar is split into sheet-like strips when the branch is freshly cut. These are divided with a knife into wide strips for spokes and narrow ones for weavers. The bark may also be shredded into soft flexible fibers to use in making coiled baskets, Part III.

USING OUTER BARK

The one-year shoots of some shrubs and trees like birch and poplar, have tough green or brown outer bark that can be split in two sections by running the point of a knife-blade down each side of the twig. These strips are used for Twining or Simple Weaving, or in bundles for coiled basketry.

CEDAR BARK KINDLING BASKET—Figure 39

This rugged basket of brownish-red cedar bark, has a woodsy look standing beside an open fire full of kindling ready to coax along a tardy blaze. In summer it is handy for porch magazines.

Base and Sides—Fasten twelve strips of thick bark 40 inches long and $\frac{3}{8}$ inch wide to a wooden block 15 x 6 inches, A. Interlace these with spokes, B, 30 inches long. To weave sides, bend double a long bark strand, $\frac{1}{8}$ inch wide; start Pairing around spokes close to base, D. When back to first spoke, do not join but weave spirally upward, E, with rows $\frac{3}{4}$ inch apart. Make basket 9 inches high.

Border—In keeping with the basket's simple structure. Place a strip of bark, $\frac{3}{8}$ inches wide, shaded, F, horizontally in back of spokes at top of weaving. Tie narrow bark fiber around it, shown black, G; bring it out between first two spokes, Nos. 1 and 2. Keep repeating two following simple steps. STEP 1: Wrap fiber up between first two spokes and down around back splint, bringing it out between next two spokes, Nos. 2 and 3, as at H. STEP 2: Bend down left spoke No. 1, over to right, in front of narrow wrapping fiber and back splint, but in back of all standing spokes, as at I. Keep wrapping fiber up between same two spokes it came through, down around back splint, and out between next two spokes, turning left spoke over it but back of other spokes, as at J and K.

Handles—Cut two tough strips of bark 7 inches long. Bore holes in ends, slip a fine strand through, tie to sides of basket, wrap the strand over it and fasten at other side.

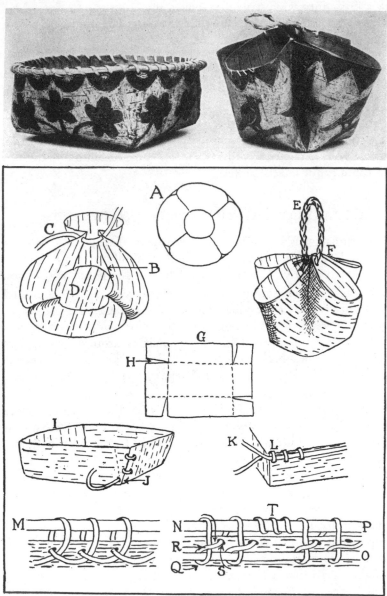

FIGURE 40—BIRCH BARK BASKETS, BARK BORDERS

The decoration on birch-bark baskets is made by scratching off with a knife the outer white bark coating. The bark should not be stripped from living trees; stripping injures the tree besides spoiling its appearance. Plenty of bark is available from dead trees. On the bark draw with pencil a simple design—flowers, birds, any motif from Nature—as a guide; then, beginning at the outer edges of the design and working inward, scrape off the bark with a knife.

The basket at the right, convenient for carrying water or sap, nuts or berries, is made of a circular piece of bark marked into quarters, Figure 40, A, with circle at center designating base. Crease straight division lines inward, as at B, draw four creases together and fasten them at top with a tough fiber, as at C; make fastening stitches by sewing in and out with bark strip. The center, D, forms base. Braid handle, E, insert through top points, F, and tie ends together.

The birch bark tray at left may be used for fruits, breads or sewing. It is made of a square or oblong piece of bark, G, with cutouts taken at each corner, as far into bark as depth of basket is to be, as shown at H. Bend sides upward into box form I, and sew corners together with narrow strips of bark, J, tucking cut ends under corners. To finish top, measure splint or thick piece of bark, K, long enough to go around basket, and sew it around top edge with over-and-over stitches, L.

BARK BORDERS—Figure 40

The edges of baskets made of flat bark may be finished with buttonhole stitch, illustrated at Figure 40, M, or with wrapping stitch, as at N. Bark is shown shaded.

For button-hole border at M, lay rod parallel to edge of bark and above it; bind it to bark with fibrous strand using button-hole stitch. Edge of stitches may lie either along top of rod, or along outside of bark, as shown here.

To make wrapped border at N, lay round rod, O, parallel to and just below edge; and lay a second rod, P, also parallel to and just above edge. Tie these rods to bark with wrappings of sewing strand. Fasten strand at a corner on inside of basket; carry it over top rod from back to front, as at N, arrow; down over and up under lower rod as at Q; out from behind lower rod and across its own stitch, as at R; and finally in through bark, as at S, and back of top rod again. Take these fastening stitches in groups of two, and in between them wrap sewing strand around top rod several times, as at T.

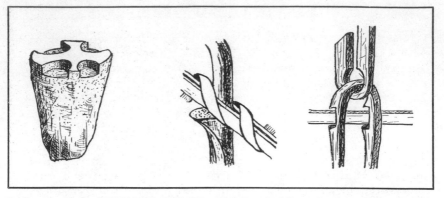

FIGURE 41—*Left*, MOHEGAN POTATO STAMP. *Middle*, HANDLE WITH SHELF UNDER BORDER, CARVED FROM THE HEART-WOOD OF A BRANCH. *Right*, CARVED HANDLE OF TWO INTERLOCKING LOOPS OF WOOD

CHAPTER XV

SPLINT BASKETS

THE early colonists knew the value of trees the bark of which could be split into weaving strips. They made constant use of ash, hickory, oak and maple to make "splint baskets." The word "splints" came to mean especially the flat white strips obtained from a few much used trees, although they are regular strips of split bark.

Splints are used for both plaited and woven·baskets, either alone or in combination with weaving fillers such as sweet grass. They make strong scrap baskets, wood baskets, clothes baskets, flat trays and carrying baskets. Splint knitting baskets and covered work baskets of our great grandmothers were necessary parts of household furnishings. There were always plenty of black ash trees from which to obtain splints of convenient thickness to make baskets for every necessity. The early settlers may have copied some of these from the Indians who often entered their villages in groups loaded down with splint baskets to trade or sell. We still find some of the Indian splint baskets in old attics decorated with patches of color, no longer bright but showing the crude design of a stamped pattern on the surface of the splints. The Indians cut designs into the flat ends of potatoes and used these "potato stamps" the way we use a block print, probably with vegetable dyes. A drawing of an actual potato stamp is shown in Figure 41.

Stamping splint baskets may still be a delightful project, using batik dyes or India inks to paint over the cut potato surface before taking each impression.

OBTAINING AND PREPARING SPLINTS

The best logs for splitting are those that have lain in the moist woods or been soaking in a pool for a month or more to loosen their layers. The outer bark is first removed from the log. The worker then pounds along its entire length with a flat heavy hammer or the pole of an ax, tapping back and forth for a time to loosen a strip of bark near the surface. Then with the blade of the ax or a knife he pries loose and peels off a bark layer. It may be wide or narrow and usually ⅟₁₆ to ⅛ inch thick. After removing all the strips that come off easily, the worker pounds loose a second layer. When he has stripped off all the layers down to the heartwood, he turns the log over and peels splints from the other side. The tough heartwood is whittled into handle rods, or half-rounds for the rims of baskets.

The strips are usually cut into various widths, dried and stored for future use. Their surface is rubbed smooth with sandpaper or shaved by running a knife over the strips with its blade slanting forward toward the worker. Splints may be dyed any color by boiling in regular cloth dyes, and splint baskets may be brushed with wood stains to give them darker wood tones.

The secret of making good splint baskets is to cut the splints an even width, (a marking gauge from the hardware store will measure off lines for cutting) render their surface smooth, and soak them until pliable before using. Start splint work with a simple basket like the square desk tray at Figure 61, R.

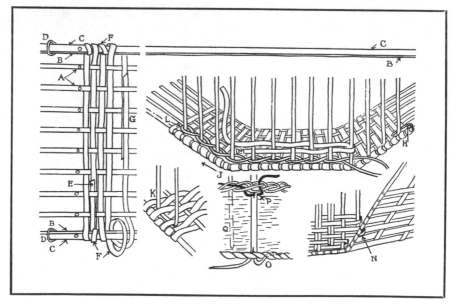

FIGURE 42—A GRACEFUL FLOWER-GATHERING BASKET DESIGNED TO
ACCOMMODATE LONG STEMS

Never fight shy of a new kind of basket. This basket for long flower stems looks difficult, but it is easy if followed step by step.

Materials—Spokes, No. 4. Weavers, thin ash splints ¼ inch wide. Side edges of base, two pieces No. 5, and strong copper wire. Handle, No. 7 and No. 5.

Base—Interweave parallel spokes, A, with a flexible weaver. Tack two pieces No. 5 reed, 26 inches long, parallel to each other and 8 inches apart on a board, C. Lay copper wire, same length, on inside of each, B, then nail spraddle tacks over both wire and reed, D. Cut nine spokes, A, of No. 4 reed 36 inches long and lay at even intervals between C-spokes, tacking them down 7 inches from their ends.

Use thin well soaked splints for weaving; start close to tacks and conceal end, E, back in weaving. Each time across take extra turn around side spoke and wire, F. Piece as at G, laying new end under last two inches of old weaver. Weave until basket measures 22 x 8 inches. Bend wire at ends, H, down over finished weaving to keep it from unraveling. Bend end parts of wire upward to form raised ends, J, leaving 6 inches at center of base for basket to rest on. At basket edges, K, insert spokes of No. 4 reed, 24 inches long, bending each spoke at its center and slipping between upper and lower strands of weaving. To hold these spokes upright, weave row of Pairing with No. 3 around all four edges, as at L, going along one side, across first end, along other side and back across opposite end to start.

Sides—Begin in-and-out weaving with splint, M; fill in side sections between bent up ends of base, reversing around spokes at end of each row. If no spoke is at this point, slip strand through weaving, N. When sides come to level with bent up ends of base finish top with a Pairing row all around basket.

Border—Clip off ends of large side reeds next to wires, at H, and replace with No. 4 spokes inserted at four corners. Use Closed Border No. 2 (Figure 12).

Handle—There are four handle rods. For the two thick outer ones, whittle two pieces No. 7 reed, 35 inches long, flat at ends; insert through border on outside of basket 3 inches apart, pushing down through base, as at O; split their ends and conceal them in weaving. Make hole in each at point where it meets border, P, run fine flexible strand through hole and tie handle to border. Cut two inside pieces, No. 5, 30 inches long. Insert in border, at intervals of 1 inch between larger reeds; conceal ends in weaving, Q. Start winding handle 6 inches above border with two strands of fine reed, winding in and out of handle rods for 2 inches, (Figure 26), then wrapping around all four rods together across top of handle to other side, and finishing with in-and-out weaving similar to first side.

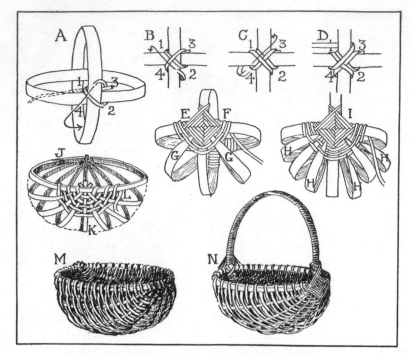

MELON-SHAPED CARRYING BASKET—FIGURE 43, N

This melon-shaped carrying basket is built on a foundation of two embroidery hoops or two spliced splints either round or oval.

Fastening Hoops—Start basket as at A, crossing hoops at right angles. If oval, cross at their narrow ends to make a shallow basket with low handle; along their wide sides to make a deep basket with high handle. Label opposite diagonal corners 1 and 2, 3 and 4.

To fasten hoops together, start narrow splint weaver in back of vertical hoop with its long end coming out at corner 1, as at dotted lines.

First step, A. Carry weaver across intersection from corner 1 to 2; pass it upward, back of horizontal hoop to corner 3; then follow curving arrow for second step. Fasten short end under crossing.

Second step, B. Carry weaver across intersection from corner 3 to 4; pass it back of vertical hoop to corner 2; follow curving arrow for third step.

Third step, C. Carry weaver across intersection from corner 2 to 1; pass it back of horizontal hoop to corner 4; follow curving arrow for fourth step.

Fourth step, D. Carry weaver across intersection from corner 4 to 3; pass it back of vertical hoop to corner 1, the starting point.

This first wrapping around each splint fastens hoops securely. For effective pattern center continue with four or five similar rounds, each time laying weaver a little further to outside of central crossing to give concentric effect at E. Last round finishes at corner 1.

Weaving Melon Shape—Carry weaver from corner 1, down over horizontal hoop and under and over splints from E to F. For extra spokes, insert two splints, same width as hoops and whittled at ends, between main hoops, G; weave back and forth in half circle between these five lower spokes. After several rows, insert four more spokes between first five, H, and weave under and over these nine, I, to bottom of basket.

Start opposite side of basket in same way; insert splint ends used on first side into weaving, adjusting them to form smooth basin-like curve under basket. Piece weavers of both sides where they meet by running their ends in-and-out of same splints for several inches. Leave handle plain or wrap with a flat strand, N.

MELON-SHAPED BASKET WITHOUT HANDLE—
FIGURE 43, M

A half-round basket without a handle made over a heavy wooden ring and woven with tough vines will be found attractive and useful in many ways—to hold bundles of mending, pop corn, nuts, apples, or kindling. Directions for making it are practically the same as those given for the melon basket with handle.

The basket measures 16 inches in diameter and is 8 inches deep. The horizontal ring is a heavy spliced splint, the spokes and weavers, willow or vines. For foundation ring, cut a heavy splint or piece of flexible wood 50 inches long and ¾ inch wide; splice ends, glue and nail, J. Cut seven to nine lower spokes of willow 24 inches long. Place vertical one first, K, with its ends coming just above top of foundation ring; gradually add other spokes, following directions for weaving lower part of melon basket above, E to H. Use flexible weaver, L; insert additional spokes to make weaving closer.

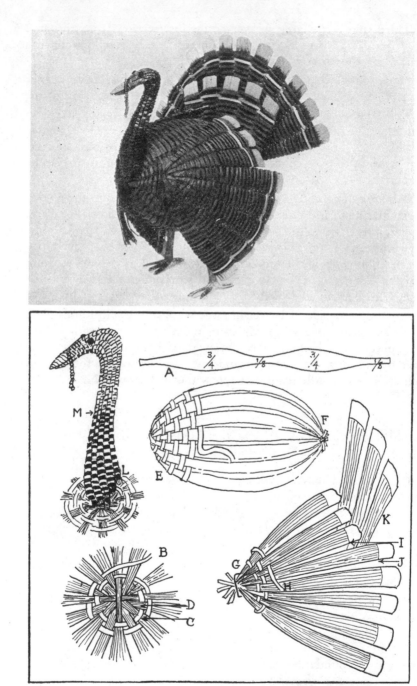

Figure 44—BASKET TURKEY OF BLACK AND NATURAL ASH SPLINTS

[92]

This little black and white turkey of ash splints shows the possibility of our native basketry materials for making quaint animal figures.

Materials—Spokes, ash splints, ¾ inch wide for body, wings and tail; ⅛ inch wide for head. Weavers, splints ⅛ inch wide for body and wings; for head, splints ¹⁄₁₆ inch wide and some red and yellow raffia. Dye some weavers black; paint spokes with black dye to within ½ inch of ends.

Body—Whittle eight spokes 10 inches long into shape at A, ⅛ inch wide at center, ¾ inch wide midway between ends and center, and ⅛ inch wide at ends. Cross eight spokes at centers, as at B. Weave in-and-out with ⅛ inch weaver, passing over top spokes, C, under lower spokes, D. Clip off one spoke leaving fifteen ends, so as to use one weaver. Bend spokes in melon-shaped body, E, 4 inches thick at center, tapering gradually to back, F. Fasten with raffia.

Wings—For side wings, G, cut five 5 inch splints, ¾ inch wide, and three 4 inch splints, ¾ inch wide; trim front ends to points. Lay parallel with three short spokes above, cross points, tack down to board as at G, then weave back and forth with strand ⅛ inch wide, as at H. Finish short spokes ½ inch from ends, as at I; continue long ones to ½ inch from ends, as at J. Soak G tips, bend under wing, insert into sides and fasten with raffia.

Tails—Make two tails like wings, one with twelve spokes 5 inches long, one with five spokes 3 inches long, all of them ¾ inch wide tapering to ⅛ inch at one end. Insert between wings, as at K, slipping ends like G across tied back, F; fasten with raffia.

Head—Insert nine spokes ⅛ inch wide at center front, around in circle, L; weave in-and-out of them with ¹⁄₁₆ inch weaver for 2 inches to M. Change to red raffia weaver; weave 2 inches more. Soak spokes, bend over for head, trim to points, weave head 1 inch long. For upper bill, wrap half the spokes in a solid group with yellow raffia; for lower bill trim rest of spokes a little shorter and wrap tight.

Feet—Whittle feet from heartwood of an ash branch; split lower ends in half; carve spur out of back half, and three toes out of front half.

FIGURE 45—STORAGE BASKET OF WILLOW COILS

STORAGE BASKET OF WILLOW COILS—FIGURE 45

Charming in texture and woodsy looking, yet simply made is this dark brown storage basket using bunches of flexible willow withes both for foundation coil and for fastening coils together. Use twigs of willow picked during summer, leaving both bark and leaves on them, and soak until pliable in a large tub of water before coiling. Start the center as in Figure 47, J, with several leafy rods for the foundation. Use a small group of flexible withes for sewing coils together, preparing a hole for each stitch by pushing a pointed stick of wood through preceding row. Keep the thickness of the coil even by adding more willow rods on the inside of basket, and narrow the coils toward top to make the graceful shape shown, considered convenient by the Indians for storing their grain. The basket measures 3 feet across base, 3 feet high and 1½ feet across top. Other flexible materials may be used.

[94]

PART III—
FLEXIBLE BASKETRY MATERIALS

CHAPTER XVI

THE CHARACTER OF COILED WORK

"For thus the tale was told
By a Penobscot woman
As she sat weaving a basket,
A basket or abaznoda
Of that sweet-scented grass
Which Indians dearly love."
—CHARLES LELAND

IN wicker baskets, Parts I and II, the basket framework is made up of many spokes; in coiled baskets it consists only of a single flexible rod that coils round and round a starting circle. Each coil is sewed to the last one with a fine tough fiber—the sewing strand. In wicker baskets there are spokes and weavers; in coiled baskets, the foundation coil and the sewing strand. Sometimes a colored strip of bark or a glossy grass blade is laid over and sewed in with the foundation rod. This, called an overlay strand, is used to make a basket pattern. In the lower basket of Figure 54 light overlay strands are used for background, dark for the butterfly design.

Sewed baskets may be as tiny as a thimble, made of barks or roots shredded to thread-like fibers; some look like needlework embroidery, soft enough to crush in the hand, for instance, the sea-grass baskets of the Aleutian Islands. Cone-shaped Indian hats are coiled baskets sewed with fine fibers, row upon row. Indeed the soft straw hats of many native peoples are really inverted coiled or plaited baskets, like the famous "Panama," woven under water. Large coarse baskets, too, are made with the same method of coiling,—great basin-like food trays, and storage baskets as big as barrels. A beautiful one in Figure 45 is made of thick bundles of willow twigs sewed together with fine withes.

Coiled baskets may be almost any shape,—round, square, oval, or of curving contour,—mats, basin-like placques, long oval trays, round sewing baskets, cylindrical storage baskets, tall graceful vase forms, beautifully rounded water jugs. Stripes or patterns are made by changing the color of the sewing strand or overlay. Sometimes the foundation shows through and adds a background of color.

[95]

The Foundation Material—Must be pliable yet strong enough to give body to the basket; it may be a single rod, several used together as one, or a bundle of split rods. Vines, most all first-year shoots like willow, cottonwood, and poplar; narrow flat strips of bark or root; and clusters of straw, stems or midribs of leaves, bundles of grass or rush, pine needles, corn husks, shredded yucca leaves, cane, cat-tails, flags, even stalks of oats, rye and wheat,— all are useful and beautiful foundation material.

The Sewing Strand—Must be tough enough to hold the coils together yet pliable enough to sew with. Good sewing materials are fibrous grasses, rushes, the veins of stripped leaves or ferns, split inner barks, split roots,—dark maidenhair fern stems, split red cedar, willow, oak and ash, strands of black or white sedge root, split cat-tails. Weak fibers may be twisted together into a strong twine-like strand while working.

The Indian still prepares split roots from many woody shrubs and trees, like spruce and elm, to sew gambling baskets and placques. First he splits a strand away from the root heartwood, puts one end between his teeth, pulls the other end taut with the left hand, and scrapes its sides smooth with a knife held in the right. When the thread is reduced to a satisfactory fineness and polish, he soaks it in water until pliable.

The Overlay—Should be colorful, thin and flexible. Use flat glossy straws, split leaves, grass stems, cane, strips of cherry bark, cedar bast and split stems of the maidenhair fern.

Tools—The only tools necessary are a knife and an awl; the knife for splitting, whittling and cutting; the awl for making holes for new stitches. The Indian uses a bone awl because it gently wedges its way between fibers without breaking them. He sharpens his sewing strand to a point and inserts it through the hole made by the awl—his needle. The modern basket worker may need scissors and needle.

Gathering Materials—Most flexible materials are best gathered in mid-summer when their growth is full but before they have become hard. Marsh-growing plants like rush and cat-tails should be gathered in early spring, split while green, then dried. Do not use any material in its green state; it will shrink and leave gaps in your finished basket. Dry the strands in an attic or on a rack out of doors, turning over now and then for even drying. Choose a shady place to make them green-gray, a sunny spot to give them tones of brown and tan. Dry grasses a week or so, thicker materials longer. Hang in a dry place; soak before using and wrap in a moist towel.

Chapter XVII

WEAVING WITH FLEXIBLE BASKETRY MATERIALS

I N weaving with flexible basketry materials, we learn first how to make starts or coiling centers; second, how to make coiling stitches for basket sides; and third, various kinds of borders to finish off the coiling.

1. COILED BASKETRY CENTERS

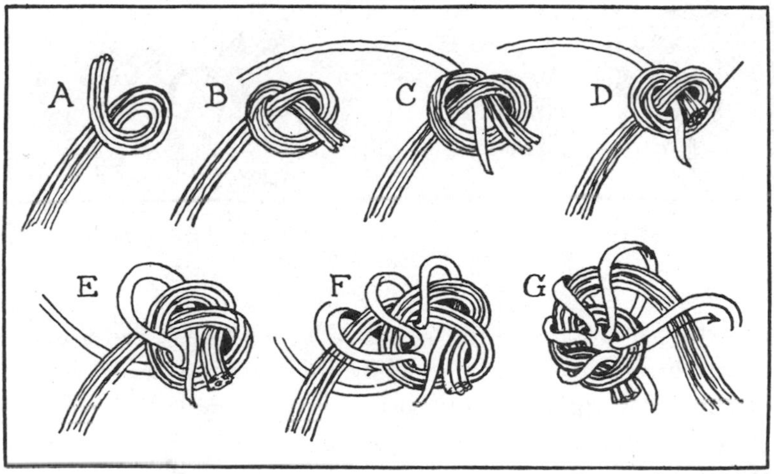

Courtesy of Gene Weltfish

FIGURE 46—KNOT START FOR COILING

Knot Start For Coiling, Figure 46—A simple way to start a coiled center is to make a knot of the foundation material. First lay the strands together in a bundle and make a loop with their short ends, A; then bring short ends up through loop, B. Next, insert sewing strand through loop, C; pull knot taut, D; and clip ends of foundation material close to center, arrow. Wrap sewing strand through center and around knot, E. Take over-and-over stitches all around knot for first row of coiling, F, then begin second row with any coiling stitch. If the worker stitches from right to left, continue direction of stitches shown at F. If worker prefers stitching from left to right, turn work over, as at G, and follow course of stitches shown at G, arrow.

[97]

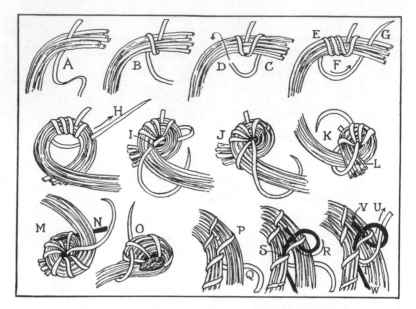

FIGURE 47—STARTING A COILED GRASS CENTER. *Below right*, PIECING
THE SEWING STRAND

Starting a Coiled Grass Center, Figure 47

—When a bundle
of many grasses makes up the coiling foundation of a basket, start
its center by wrapping a short portion of the bundle with a flexible
sewing strand, then bend it into a loop or coil. Hold bundle in
left hand with short ends pointed to right, and insert sewing
strand up through them, A. Wrap strand over and around bundle
at left of sewing end, B; then wrap it over and around part of
bundle at right, C. Bring strand to left again, arrow, D; wrap it
around bundle three or four times, E; then carry it under all wrappings, F, and up through ends at right, G. Pull sewing strand
taut, H, bending short ends under long portion in a loop.

Take first stitch around crossing of short and long ends. Bring
strand up through center, arrow, I. Pass it around coil at crossing
and bring it up through center again, J. From underneath coil,
this step appears as at K. Clip off short ends close to center, L.

From step J, continue to bind long portion of bundle to center
with sewing strand, as at M. When first round is complete, work
can proceed with any coiling stitch used over bundles of fibers
(Figures 49, 50). The simplest coiling stitch is shown here continuing the coil. Insert awl or needle through preceding coil, as

[98]

at N, entering it through loop of stitch directly underneath, and also through part of bundle at this point, as shown by black awl. Bring sewing strand up through opening made by awl. From underneath coil, this stitching appears as at O, with strand coming through stitch in last row and section of bundle.

Piecing the Sewing Strand, Figure 47—The most practical way of piecing the end of an old sewing strand to a new one, is shown in the three diagrams at lower right of Figure 47. Learn this method so thoroughly you will not avoid piecing short lengths. It may be used for most coiling stitches whether the foundation be a rod, a splint, or a bundle of fibers. The old end and the new strand are tied together on the under side of the work, and the knot, when pulled tight, slips in between the two rows, where it is hidden from view. The three diagrams show the piecing underneath the coil.

Turn coil upside down. At P, the old end, after its last stitch, lies across unsewed end of bundle on right side, as at Q. Slip new end (shaded in diagram) under last stitch from right to left on wrong side, as at R; bring other end of new strand around in a loop; pass it under its own short end; and insert it through same hole made in lower row by last stitch, as at S. Lastly, bring end of old strand up between coils, as at T, and thread it through loop made by new end, as at U. By pulling tightly on old end at U and short end of new strand at V, a firm knot is formed that slips in between coils and out of sight. Clip off ends. The new strand, now taking the place of old end at its last stitch, is ready to continue coiled work at W.

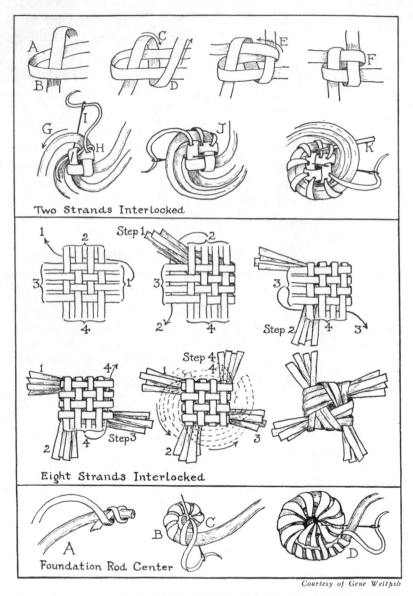

Two Strands Interlocked

Eight Strands Interlocked

Foundation Rod Center

FIGURE 48—*Above*, INTERLOCKED CENTER OF TWO STRANDS OR GROUPS OF STRANDS. *Middle*, PLAITED CENTER OF EIGHT STRANDS. *Below*, STARTING A CENTER OVER A FOUNDATION ROD

Interlocked Center of Two Strands or Groups of Strands; Figure 48, above—This center consists of two strands or bundles of strands folded together. Choose two flat flexible strands of even width (or two bundles of fibers). Fold first strand, A, double, lay its loop at left, and insert second strand, B, up through it. Loop B downward, arrow C, in back of two A ends, then carry it up over them, D. Bend upper end of first strand back to left through loop just made by second strand, as at E. Pull all four ends up taut to made locked center, F. Make foundation coil by curving all four ends around center, arrow G. Insert sewing strand through plaiting, as at H, and begin sewing four ends to center, as at I. Continue all around as at J. Start second round with any coiling stitch, as at K. If worker prefers sewing from left to right, coil starting ends around clockwise.

Plaited Center of Eight Strands, Figure 48, middle—This start is used by the Pima Indians of Arizona to make flat centers for coiled baskets. Although it appears difficult, it is solved, like most Indian processes, simply. Begin by interlacing four strands with four similar ones at right angles to them, first drawing. Label groups of strands coming out from sides of plaited square, edges 1, 2, 3, and 4. Fold each of these groups in succession under plaited center as follows:

Step 1: Bunch together four strands of edge 1; bend them behind and across strands of edge 2; bring them out at upper left corner, 1.

Step 2: Bunch together four strands of edge 2; bend them behind and across edge 3 (also passing under ends at corner 1); bring them out at corner 2.

Step 3: Bunch together four strands of edge 3; bend them behind and across edge 4 (also passing under ends at lower left corner 2); bring them out at corner 3.

Step 4: Bunch together four strands of edge 4; bend them behind edge 1 and through loop made by first group (also passing under ends at lower right corner, 3); bring them out at upper right corner, 4.

The diagram at Step 4 shows the finished center; last drawing shows the center from beneath. To start first row of coiling, bend strands of each corner around center, dotted lines, and start sewing foundation coil thus made to plaited center. For a fine coil, trim some strands away.

Starting a Center Over a Foundation Rod, Figure 98, below—Wrap a sewing strand around the narrow end of a flexible rod for 1 inch, A. Bend wrapped end around in a coil, B, and start taking stitches through center and around unwrapped end of foundation rod, as at C. Make one complete round with stitches through center; begin second round, D, with any coiling stitch, Figures 49, 50, B, C, D, E, F, H, K, L; Figure 51, A, B.

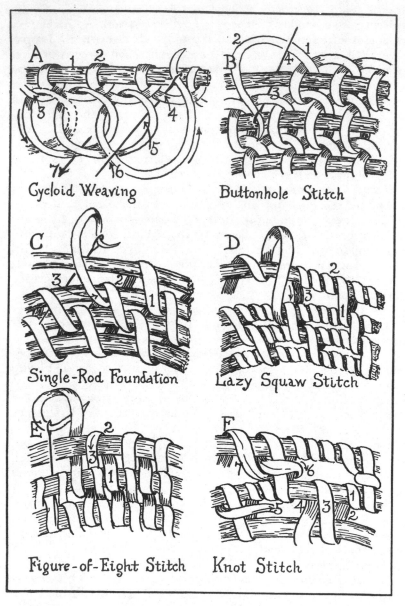

A — Cycloid Weaving

B — Buttonhole Stitch

C — Single-Rod Foundation

D — Lazy Squaw Stitch

E — Figure-of-Eight Stitch

F — Knot Stitch

FIGURE 49—COILING STITCHES

2. COILING STITCHES—Figures 49, 50

Coiled Work Without a Foundation, or Cycloid Weaving, Figure 49,
A—This stitch, worked from the top downward, is used for openwork
bags and lacy baskets. Make a flexible ring for top of basket, 1. Form a
row of half-loops, 2, over ring; start first row of whole loops over them,
3. For each stitch, carry strand to right of last stitch, counter-clockwise, 4, under next half-loop and under the stitch, 4 to 5, and out over
its own loop, 6. Take stitches of next row around single loops of row
above, or over two loops at a time, arrow 7.

Fuegian or Button-hole Stitch, Figure 49, B—The Fuegian Indians of
South America use this stitch over several rush or grass strands to weave
delicate baskets, with soft foundation colors showing through the meshes.
Start basket like Figures 46 or 47. Bring sewing strand out from under
coil, B, 1; throw strand to left in a loop, 2; insert it up under next loop
to left in lower coil, and also under the upper foundation rod, 3; carry
it over its own loop, 4, ready for next stitch.

Single Rod Foundation With Simple Coiling, Figure 49, C—In this
stitch, the sewing strand wraps around both new and old coil, and also
interlocks with stitches of old coil. Bring sewing strand out from under
foundation rod of last row, C, 1; carry it up over, and down in back of,
both upper and lower rods, 2; insert it through next stitch in lower row,
passing under rod at this point, 3.

Lazy Squaw Stitch, Figure 49, D—Like Simple Coiling, C, with wrappings in between stitches. Bring sewing strand out from beneath old
coil, D, 1; carry it up over new coil, 2; wrap it around new coil several
times; carry it down behind both coils; insert it through next stitch of
lower coil and under foundation rod at this point, 3.

Figure-eight Stitch, Figure 49, E—The sewing strand fastens the new
to the old coil by twisting around them like a figure-eight. Bring sewing strand out from under last row and between two stitches of last
row, E, 1; carry it up over lower rod and behind upper rod, 2; then down
in front of upper rod and under lower rod, passing between stitches, 3.

Knot Stitch, Figure 49, F—Called also "knot of Mariposa" from the
Mariposan Indians of the west, unexcelled basket makers. Three different
stitches are shown here to describe one complete stitch. First bring sewing strand out from beneath upper coil, F, 1; wrap it down in back of
both coils, 2; up and over both coils, 3; and out between upper and
lower coils, 4. Second, wrap it to right over this double stitch, 5. Third,
carry it around in back of stitch, 6; and bring it out between upper
and lower coils, 7, ready for next wrapping around both coils. The
knots may be taken close together or with wrappings between.

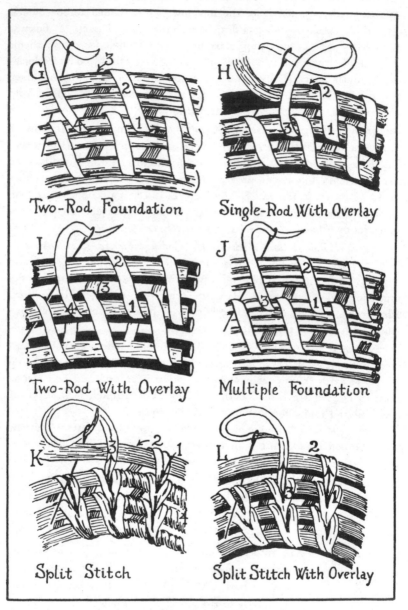

G Two-Rod Foundation

H Single-Rod With Overlay

I Two-Rod With Overlay

J Multiple Foundation

K Split Stitch

L Split Stitch With Overlay

FIGURE 50—COILING STITCHES, Continued

Two-Rod Foundation, Figure 50, G—Like Simple Coiling, C, with each coil made up of two rods instead of one, the stitch passing under the upper rod only of lower coil while attaching new coil. Bring sewing strand out from under top rod of last row, G, 1; carry it up over this rod and over two rods of upper row, 2; then down in back of them, 3; lastly insert it under upper rod of old coil, 4.

Single-Rod Foundation With Overlay, Figure 50, H—Like Simple Coiling, C, except that a strip of overlay covers the foundation and is included in the stitch. The sewing strand passes only under overlay material of last row if this is strong enough to hold. Bring sewing strand out from under overlay of last row, H, 1; carry it up over this overlay and also over and in back of upper rod and its overlay, 2; then insert it through next stitch in lower row and under overlay of lower row at this point, 3.

Two-Rod Foundation With Overlay, Figure 50, I—Like Single-Rod Overlay, H, except that the foundation consists of two parallel rods and the overlay lies between them and partly over both, covering up the gap. Bring sewing strand out from under overlay of lower coil, I, 1; carry it up over rest of lower coil, over two rods and overlay of upper coil, 2; around in back of them, 3; then insert it under overlay material of lower coil, interlocking with stitch at this point, 4.

Multiple Foundation of Several Rods, Figure 50, J—Several rods are in the foundation coil and the stitch is usually taken under the upper one only of the lower coil. Bring sewing strand out from beneath topmost rod of lower coil, J, 1; carry it up and over rest of bundle, over and in back of entire upper coil, 2; then insert it through next stitch of lower coil and under top rod or rods of coil at this point, 3.

Split or Furcate Stitch, Figure 50, K—The splitting of stitches was at first accidental; later it became the means of a beautiful basket ornamentation. The stitch is taken directly through the center of the stitch beneath instead of under it or beside it. Bring sewing strand out from under rod of last row and through middle of stitch at this point, K, 1; carry it over and in back of upper coil, 2; insert it through middle of next stitch in lower coil and under foundation at this point, 3. Split stitches may be taken close together or with wrappings between.

Split Stitch With Overlay, Figure 50, L—This overlay stitch is like that at H, with split stitches holding the coils together, instead of simple coiling stitches. Bring sewing strand out from under overlay of last row and through middle of stitch, L, 1; carry it up over this overlay and also over and back of upper rod and its overlay, 2; then insert it through center of next stitch in lower row and under overlay at this point, 3. The split stitch may also pass completely through stitch, overlay, and foundation material at the same time; in this case insert needle from front to back.

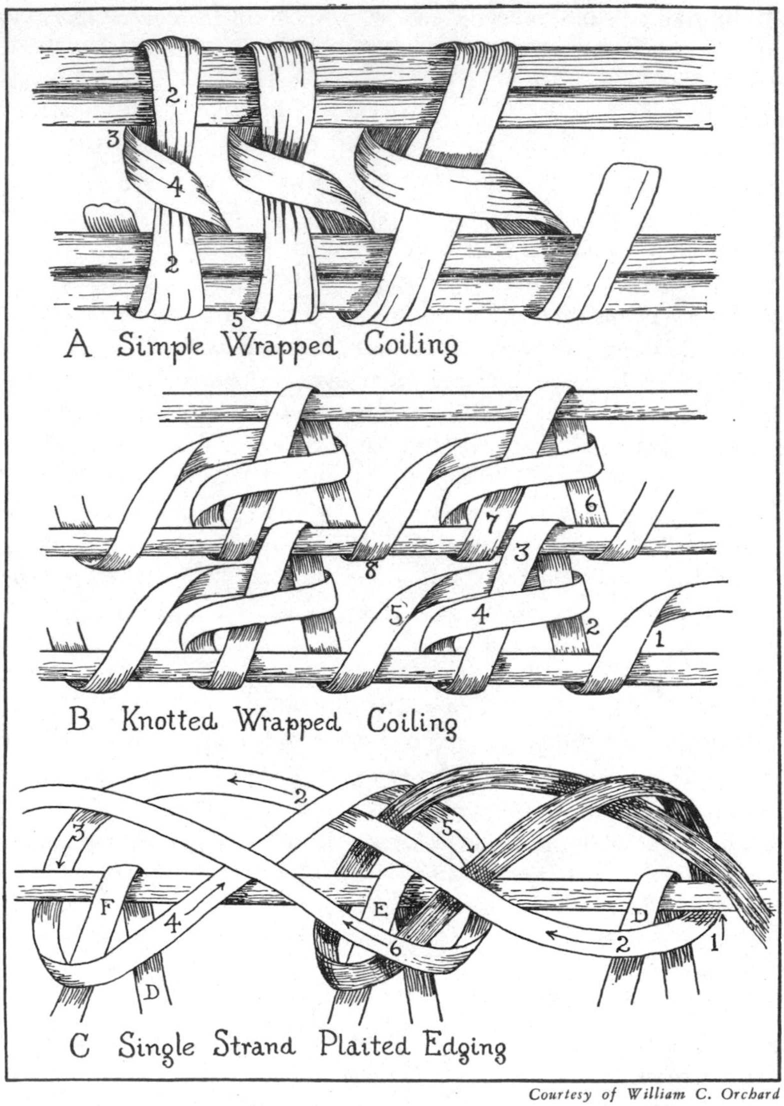

A Simple Wrapped Coiling

B Knotted Wrapped Coiling

C Single Strand Plaited Edging

FIGURE 51—TWO WRAPPED COILING STITCHES AND A PLAITED BORDER

Simple Wrapped Coiling, Figure 51, A—In this stitch a twist is taken around each coiling stitch; the foundation may be one rod or several; the stitches pass between each two of the last row. Start with a fastening around lower coil, 1; carry strand up over both lower and upper coils, 2; bring it out from beneath upper coil at left of stitch, 3; loop strand in front of stitch, from left to right, 4; and carry it down in back of lower coil and out to front ready for next stitch, 5. To work stitch from right to left, interchange words "right" and "left" in above directions.

Knotted Wrapped Coiling, Figure 51, B—A decorative, yet secure stitch. Tie sewing strand to coil, B, 1; carry strand up in back of lower and upper coils, 2; down in front of both coils, 3; up and out between coils at left of stitch, 4; make a loop around stitch from front to back, 4 to 5, bringing strand out between rods ready for next stitch; pull knot taut. The stitch falls into three parts: up and under both rods; down and over both rods; and a knot around this double stitch. In next row, take upward wrapping, 6, at right of stitch below, and downward wrapping, 7, at its left. To widen basket insert new knots between stitches, at midpoints like 8. To work from left to right, interchange words "right" and "left" in above directions.

3. BORDERS FOR COILED WORK

Coiled baskets may be finished with a row of the same weaving used for basket, tapering the foundation down to a level with last row.

A colored border is formed by wrapping the top row or rows with close wrappings of a colored strand over the regular stitches.

Buttonhole stitching also forms a convenient edge, Figure 52, C.

In addition to the above, two excellent borders are shown in Figure 51, C, and Figure 52, A, B.

Single Strand Braid Border, Figure 51, C—This border consists of two long stitches taken back and forth at successive intervals over top row. Start wrapping strand under top row, arrow 1. Follow numbers to left, disregarding shaded loop of preceding stitch.

For first long stitch, carry strand up in a loop over top row to left, arrow 2, skipping three coiling stitches of basket, D, E and F; insert strand under foundation of top row from back to front at left of third stitch, F, as at 3.

For second long stitch, carry strand up over top row to right, arrow 4, skipping two stitches only, E and F; insert sewing strand under foundation from back to front at right of second stitch, arrow 5.

Continue as at 6, passing strand over three stitches to left, then under foundation; back over two stitches to right, then under foundation. Fasten sewing strand under last stitch.

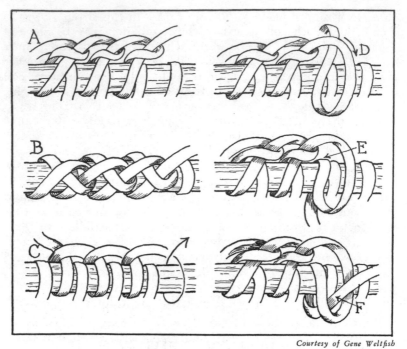

FIGURE 52—LOOPED BRAID EDGE

Looped Braid Edge—This delightful braid edge was recently discovered being made by a squaw called Lottie Fancy Eagle, in a Pawnee Indian tribe. From the side view at A, one can see how easily it is worked, with the same idea as a button-hole stitch. Yet it is far superior, producing an attractive braid finish with simple loops, appearing from above as at B. The regular buttonhole edge is shown at C.

To make this Pawnee braid edge, fasten long flexible strand to top row at left of work, (working either on inside or outside of basket).

First, loop strand over clockwise in front of edge, as at D.

Second, carry end down in back of row, between next two stitches and around under row, as at E.

Third, bring strand out from beneath row and insert up through its own loop, as at F. Draw up knot ready for next looped stitch. Take stitches between coiling stitches of top row of basket.

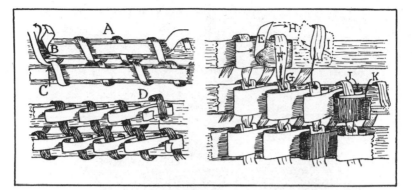

FIGURE 53—STITCHES USED FOR OVERLAY MATERIALS
A-C—Beading.   D-I—Imbricated weaving.   J-K—Piecing Overlay Patterns

Two popular methods of coiling, one called Beading, the other Imbrication, are used when an overlay is included with the foundation.

Beading, Figure 53, A—The overlay lies flat over the foundation and shows through the coiling stitches.   Use Single Rod Coiling, Figure 49, C.   Include overlay under each alternate stitch only, lifting it above every second stitch, arrow, B. The stitches may pass through foundation rod of preceding row, as well as under coiling stitches, C.

Imbricated Weaving, Figure 53, D-K—The overlay is "imbricated" or braided in as part of the stitch itself, not merely sewed over along with the foundation.   This method of adding colorful straws or bits of bark makes a strong, beautiful basket texture, Figure 54.   The stitch is shown worked from left to right; the folding of the overlay back and forth upon itself makes a kind of knife-plaiting.   The foundation must be flat or nearly so and the overlay may cover half of it, D, or all of it, E to K.

Tie overlay to foundation with sewing strand, at left of work. Lay overlay down to right over rod, and loop it back upon itself, arrow, E; take simple stitch with sewing strand over loop E from back to front, F; carry stitch down to lower row and split the stitch beneath, G, passing strand right through foundation and overlay of preceding row.   Bend overlay of upper row to right to cover stitch just taken, dotted lines, H; carry it along foundation rod and double it back upon itself again, I, ready for next stitch from back of rod downward.

Piecing Overlay Patterns, Figure 53, J-K—Piece overlay strands of contrasting colors by overlapping their ends under a loop, J. The strand of first color may be cut off behind new strand, as at K, or carried along under new strand until needed again.

FIGURE 54—TWO BEAUTIFUL IMBRICATED BASKETS USING SIMPLE
OVERLAY PATTERNS

Above, Black and yellow pattern on a basket bowl; diameter 5 inches, height 7 inches.
Below, Basket of native grasses, black design representing a butterfly

CHAPTER XVIII

PINE NEEDLE BASKETRY

"Ye lofty Pines! Ye venerable Oaks!
Ye Ashes wild, resounding o'er the steep!
Delicious is your shelter to the soul."—THOMSON.

GATHERING THE NEEDLES

PINE NEEDLES are gathered from the tree, dried out of doors to change them to a deeper richer brown, and used in bundles as foundation material in coiled baskets; they are sewed into graceful forms with the long stems of grasses or raffia. All of the pines furnish needles that may be used for this craft, but trees that have long needles are. most desirable, like the long leaved pine, *(Pinus palustris)* and the slash pine, *(Pinus carribæa)*. Young pine bushes or trees provide excellent material with needles from 12 to 20 inches long. At the time of the Civil War when materials were scarce, the southerners learned to turn these fragrant needles to many uses, one of the first being the making of a man's hat sewed round and round with thread.

The best time to gather needles is in late spring or summer, just after they have secured their full growth and before insects' eggs have been deposited on them. Pull the green needles in bunches from the tree; they grow so plentifully that you can fill a basket quickly. If there are dense pine woods in your vicinity to provide needles in abundance, break off short branches, for they are easy to dry in this state; but be sure not to harm the tree's appearance or growth. Fall is not too late to pick needles, and if one has patience and time to gather them, he will find under the trees great numbers of fallen clusters dyed by the weather a rich even brown.

CURING THE NEEDLES

We too must secure the weather's assistance in drying and dyeing the green needles or "curing" them, a process that takes a month or two. The problem is to secure a rich even color and to dry them to a point where no further shrinkage will occur after the basket is made. The needles are left out in wind and sun, frost and rain, to change to a rich golden brown. The longer they are left the darker will be their color, ranging from soft tan to deep brown. If green needles are preferred, dry them in the house away from the sun or in a shady place out of doors.

Lay the needles on a perforated surface to dry, preferably between two screens tied together where they are kept from being blown away by the wind. Turn the drying screen over now and

FIGURE 55—FRUIT BASKET OF TIED GRASSES OR RUSHES

then to secure the same amount of tanning for all the needles. After several days in the sun, the sheath on each little bunch of three or five needles shrinks and may be pulled off easily; but it does no harm to leave it on. Some lovely baskets depend upon these brown stipules for their unique charm (Figure 58). Branches of needles may be laid over a fence or a trellis, open to wind and sun. They may also be spread upon dry grass where there is no danger of mould. Turn the branches over occasionally to secure even drying.

After the needles have turned the color desired, pull them from the branches and dip them in boiling water to kill any eggs that might later hatch out and damage them. Let the needles dry, then rub them, a few at a time, between the folds of a rough towel to polish them. Tie them in bundles with the needle ends all pointing in the same direction and keep them in a dry place until needed. Before using, dip them in water a few minutes and push off the sheaths, then lay them in a damp towel to mellow during the basket making.

COLOR POSSIBILITIES

With natural colored grasses or light raffia, the needles of brown or green are attractive. However, various colored sewing strands are used to bring out their color, contrasting or blending with them. The baskets when finished and dried thoroughly may be given a coat of transparent white shellac to make them more durable, but they should never be painted.

PINE CONES

Pine cones are used as decorations on pine needle baskets. Small ones, either alone or in groups, are fastened on the sides to give the basket an artistic touch. They may be painted or left the natural color. Groups of cones painted with bright colors are used as winter bouquets in wild vine baskets. Their stems are made of brown or green twigs, glued into holes made with a gimlet under the cones.

PINE NEEDLE BASKETRY STITCHES—FIGURE 56

Pine needles are sewed into baskets with the regular coiling stitches of Figures 49, 50. Other stitches effective to use with the needles are given here. The sewing strands may be raffia, tough grasses, leaf fibers or fine bark strips.

[113]

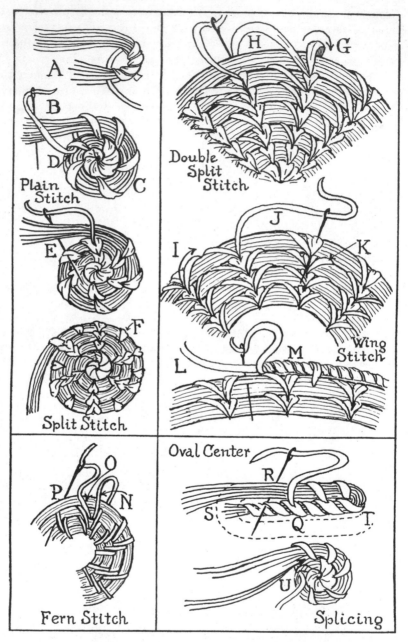

Plain Stitch

Split Stitch

Double Split Stitch

Wing Stitch

Fern Stitch

Oval Center

Splicing

FIGURE 56—PINE NEEDLE BASKETRY STITCHES

Plain Stitch, Figure 56, A—Wrap raffia around several clusters of needles, A; wind wrapped part around in a circle, B. Stitch first round through center. Continue second row, C, taking each stitch, D, through stitch just beneath it in last round, also passing through part of bundle at this point. Space stitches evenly.

Single Split Stitch, Figure 56, E—Make first and second rounds like Plain Stitch. In third round take each stitch through center of stitch beneath it, E, also passing through part of bundle at this point. Continue taking similar split stitches around spiral rows, forming radiating lines of stitches; as space widens between lines, start new stitch rows, F, midway between the old.

Double Split Stitch or Leaf Stitch, Figure 56, G—The sewing strand is inserted twice at same stitch. Start center like Plain Stitch. In third round, take split stitch at center of stitch beneath; insert strand again into same opening, G; carry it to left for next split stitch, H, finish this with second insertion, and continue.

Wing Stitch, Figure 56, I—This pretty stitch has a leaf-like extension at each side of a main split stitch. Complete one round of Double Split Stitch, G, going from right to left, making wings at left of stitches. Bring strand out at last stitch, I, and reverse its direction. Pass back over same row from left to right, J, inserting strand once only through center of each split stitch, making wings at right of stitch, K. When back to starting point, reverse again and make second row from right to left. Reverse at end of each round.

Fern Stitch, Figure 56, O—Each fern stitch is a combination of a vertical stitch, N, and a slanting stitch, O, both taken inside the V of the stitch below, around two coils. Start center as for Plain Stitch; make stitches in second round ½ inch apart. For third round take a stitch at right and one at left of stitch below. For all rounds after this take each vertical stitch, N, around coil and at left of vertical stitch, and each slanting stitch, O, around coil and at right of slanting stitch.

Borders of Pine Needle Baskets—Are similar to those for coiled baskets, Figures 51 and 52. The outer edges of pine needle baskets may be strengthened by attaching a rod or a wire to last row, Figure 56, L. Wind around wire several times, M, then take a stitch into last row, either through or between stitches below.

Oval Center, Figure 56, R—Wrap needles along straight line with sewing strand, Q; make sharp turn, bend needles back and stitch to wrapped center at short intervals, R. At opposite end, again bend needles around core, dotted lines, S, and stitch this side to center, completing first round at T. For following rounds use any type of coiling stitch.

Splicing, Figure 56, U—As bundle of needles dwindles, insert groups of three or five needles between new and old rows, U. Keep stipules on needles until needed; then clip off hard end and pull off sheaths. As basket widens, thicken coils. The bundle of a small basket should have twelve to fifteen needles, that of a large one, eighteen to twenty.

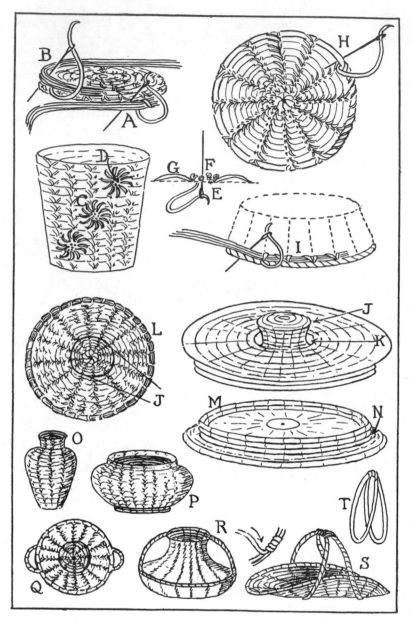

FIGURE 57—DESIGNS FOR PINE NEEDLE BASKETS

PINE NEEDLE BASKET DESIGNS

With a knowledge of the decorative stitches used for pine needles one can develop any graceful basket form.

Scrap Basket, Figure 57, A-D—Wing Stitch. Base, 8 inches. Top, 10 inches. Height, 9 inches. Start with Plain Stitch, Figure 56, B; change to Double Split Stitch over fifteen needles; form new stitch rows between old ones; press work flat on a table. Below base edge, make ledge, A, of one row; taper off level. Begin sides with new row, B; use Wing Stitch, centers 1 inch apart; make stitch-rows vertical; widen sides slightly. Decorate with black-eyed Susans, orange raffia petals, brown centers, each flower, C, 4 inches across; mark chalk outlines on basket; embroider centers, D, stitching through from underneath, E, making French knots on top, F; stitches, G, for petals. Shellac basket to make durable.

Work Basket With Lid, Figure 57, H-I—Wing Stitch. Base, 7 inches. Top, 6 inches. Height, 3 inches. Double Split Stitch Base, H; cover edge with raffia. Start sides with new small bundle, I; gradually enlarge. Use Wing Stitch, centers ¾ inch apart; make rows vertical; narrow basket to diameter of 5½ inches measuring on inside of top coil.

Lid—Start knob center, J, with fine raffia over three needles; two rows, Single Split Stitch; four rows, Wing Stitch over six needles; after sixth row, nine needles; make knob 1½ inches across. Coil rows downward ¾ inch, then outward, K; adjust flat on table. Continue with Wing Stitch over twelve needles to diameter of 6¼ inches; bind edge with raffia, L. Add rim under edge, M, its outside diameter measuring 5¼ inches, to fit inside of 5½ inch inner diameter of basket. Start ½ inch from edge, N, with Double Split Stitch; try first round into basket, adjust to fit, continue upward three rows.

Tall Vase, O—Leaf Stitch. Base, 3 inches. Widest diameter, 6 inches. Neck, 3 inches. Top, 3½ inches. Height, 9 inches. Start upward curve over a glass vase.

Low Bowl, P—Wing Stitch. Base, 4½ inches; add two rows underneath edge. Widest diameter, 9½ inches. Top, 7½ inches. Carry wire along under widest part and top for strength.

Round Tray, Q—Fern Stitch, twenty needles in bundle after start. Base, 12 inches; bind edge. Sides, three rows high if desired; insert wire under last row and bring bundle and wire out in loops to form handles; bind last row.

Flower Holder, R—Plain or Fern Stitch. Base, 4½ inches. Widest diameter, 8 inches. Neck, 3 inches. Top, 3½ inches. Height, 7 inches. Strengthen base edge and widest part with wire; bind with raffia. For handles, wires 8 inches long; conceal ends in widest row and top row, R, arrow; bind with raffia.

Fruit Basket, S—Plain or Split Stitch. Base, 12 inches; bind edge with raffia; soak, roll upward, tie with string to dry in this shape. Handles, two circles, T, of wire 26 inches around; cover with needles; wrap with raffia; bind together at top; flatten underneath basket and attach with raffia.

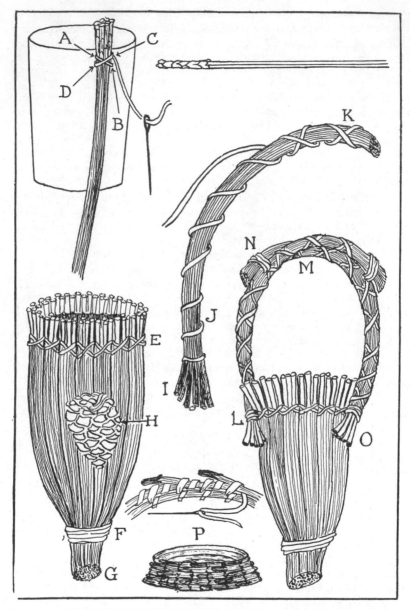

FIGURE 58—HANGING FLOWER BASKET OF LONG PINE NEEDLES WITH
SHEATHS AND CONE AS DECORATIVE NOTES

HANGING FLOWER BASKET OF LONG PINE NEEDLES—
FIGURE 58

With its soft brown pine needle color, a border of dark sheaths and its woodsy touch of a pine cone, this basket is an ideal holder for summer flowers. It measures 5 inches across top, and 11 inches high without handle which extends 5 inches above top. There is no actual basket weaving in its construction; the needles are fastened to a carton with strong raffia.

Materials—¼ pound of needles kept moist in a wet towel; ice cream carton or pasteboard cylinder a little larger than a glass tumbler to fit inside.

Border—Sew a bunch of needles with their stipules left on to top of carton with a cross, A. Knot end of a raffia sewing strand, bring out at A, in at B, out at C, in at D, and out at C again ready to attach next bunch of needles at right. Finished cross should measure ⅜ to ½ inch wide. Fasten groups of needles all around top; keep sheaths even; leave lower ends loose. Finished border appears as at E.

Base—Draw needles together below carton; fasten with a wrapped band of raffia, F, ⅝ inches wide. Trim needles off in a diagonal cut, G, 2 inches below wrapping. Attach pine cone to front with raffia stitches at head and tip.

Handle—Group two bunches of needles, with sheaths together, each bunch measuring ½ inch or more in diameter. Start wrapping with raffia next to sheaths; wrap upward in a spiral, J; reverse ½ inch from ends, K; wind back, crossing over first wrappings. When back to sheaths, make several wrappings and fasten bundle to basket border at this point, L, stitching through carton. Bring two bundles together 5 inches above border, M, and curl around each other. Trim ends off diagonally; stitch each end to other bundle with raffia, N. Notice that sheath ends of bundles, O, curve forward toward front of basket.

Shellac basket, dry thoroughly, shellac a second time to glue needles together and prevent breaking.

Small Tray, Figure 58, P—Baskets made of clusters of needles with sheaths left on are unique and ornamental. A small cuff-button tray made in this way is shown at P. Weave base with regular Plain Stitch, Figure 56, B, without sheaths. Weave sides with simple coiling stitch, Figure 49, C, inserting new clusters of needles with sheaths left on from outside of coil, leaving sheaths extending outward, as in diagram above P.

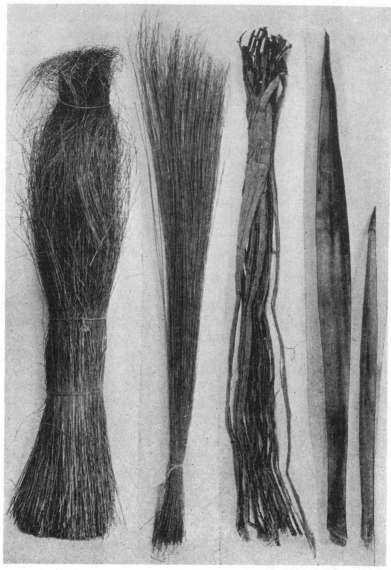

FIGURE 59—THE FIBERS WE FIND IN THE PLANT WORLD ARE UNUSU-
ALLY BEAUTIFUL IN THEIR NATURAL STATE. 1, SEDGE; 2, COMMON
RUSH; 3, PAPER MULBERRY; 4, NOLINA LEAF

CHAPTER XIX

BASKETS OF GRASSES, REEDS AND RUSHES

"A common thing is a grass-blade small,
Crushed by the feet that pass,—
But all the dwarfs and giants tall,
Working till doomsday shadows fall,
Can't make a blade of grass."—JULIAN CUTLER

GRASSES suitable for basket making are found in almost every section of the country. Most useful perhaps is the wire grass, found in lengths from 4 inches to almost 4 feet. Strong, tough, flexible and glossy, it can be worked into practical and beautiful articles that carry a suggestion of Indian and Japanese art.

Another much used grass is the sweet vernal, growing wild in many localities and highly valued by Indians for its lovely gray-green color, its flexibility and long lasting, delicate fragrance. After drying in the wind it is readily braided or twisted for use as weaving material in splint baskets where its soft color and velvety luster contrast pleasantly with the woody splints. These are left natural or dyed in bright tones of orange, flame, brown, purple, green or black.

Grasses for Coiling—Almost all grasses—wheat, straw, rye, wire grass, sweet vernal, rice grass and others—are used in bundles for foundation material, a medium size bundle having ten grass stems or "wires." The sewing strand may be raffia, fibrous grasses or finely split roots. Carry the bundles along smoothly without twisting to show the natural sheen of the grasses to the best advantage.

Split Grasses As Overlay—Grass stems when split make bright glossy overlay strips. Select young full blown stems and split them into two or three parts. Split pithy stems into three parallel parts, discard middle one and dry the two outer glossy strips to use as weavers or overlay.

Gathering and Curing Grasses—If you wish to preserve grasses in their lovely natural shades—green, straw color and even red—dry them away from the sun. Gather them when full grown in July, tie in bunches, hang them points downward in a shady place out of doors; dry thoroughly to prevent molding. For deep green, cut grasses in June; lay them in bunches under dense growths of grass for two weeks; dry them in a room with no direct sun. Some grasses, like wild rye, become ivory white after bleaching in the summer's sun. Gather these in late fall; hang them in bunches in the shade to dry. For shades of brown dry grasses in the sun. Some grasses, like wire grass, turn brown in summer. Gather these in fall; dry in the shade.

Soak grasses in cold water half an hour before using; wrap in a damp towel; warm water bleaches out their color. For future use, braid grasses and store in boxes in a dry place.

Dyeing Grasses—For touches of bright color dip grasses in concentrated cloth dyes. Tough fibrous grass stems may be boiled.

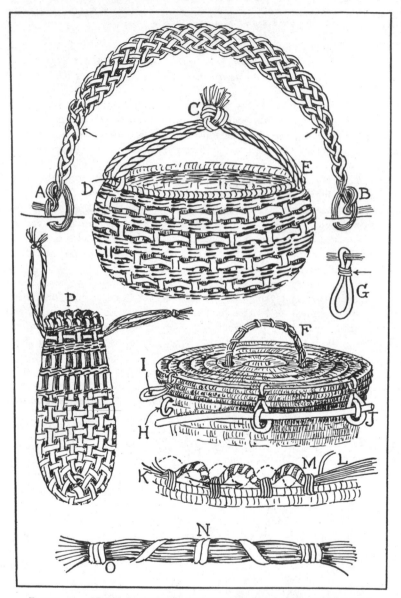

FIGURE 60—GRASS HANDLES, BORDERS, LIDS AND FASTENINGS

GRASS HANDLES, BORDERS, LIDS AND FASTENINGS—
FIGURE 60

Braided Grass Handle, A—This flat burden strap for a carrying basket is fastened to basket border at ends, A and B, and the grasses are divided into a many-strand braid at arrows; description in Figure 38. See also flat braided handle, Figure 61, M.

Twisted Grass Handle, C—In this double rope handle the ends of the grasses are knotted above the basket, C. To make one rope, loop bundle of strands around border, D; open ends out in a straight line with the border at its center, and twist from end to end, Figure 61, B. When kinks form, bend twisted strands double again and twist in opposite direction, forming a secure rope with border inside loop at its base. Make similar rope next to this one, and two at opposite side, E. Knot all four at C.

Wrapped Grass Handles, F, N—For handle at F, wrap group of grass stems with strong fibers; tie all together under lid. Include wire within bundle of grasses for extra strength. For handle at N lying flat across center of lid, bind bundle of grass strands with raffia and fasten down ends with wrappings around bundle and through lid, O.

Grass Basket Borders, K, P—The openwork border, at K, is convenient to run rope handles through. Bind down bundle of strands, L, at regular intervals to top of basket with a sewing strand, M, wrapping up over loops between fastenings. Make a double border of this type by looping a second bundle of grasses along basket edge, dotted lines, fastening them down at points between first wrappings.

Open spaces left in the weaving near the top of a basket, as at P, form an openwork border for the insertion of braided or twisted ropes. In this pouch basket the bark warp is left unwoven for $1/2$ inch.

Also use the same borders as for Coiled baskets, Figures 51, and 52; or for pine needles, Figure 56; likewise some of the borders in Figure 36.

Grass Basket Lids, F—Covers for grass baskets are made to lie either flat over the basket top as in the pine needle cover, Figure 57, or to come down over the basket edge, Figure 60, H. They may be of any shape, made like coiling centers, Figures 46, 47, 48, or like flat basketry centers, Figures 33, 34.

Fastenings, H-I—Unique fastenings for lids are made of twisted or braided loops tied to their front edges. These lock down over small sticks of carved wood, tree knots, or knobs of knotted grass stems attached to front of basket. A good fastening is shown at Fig. 60, I. Make three loops of grasses at top front edge of lid, as at G, about 2 inches long; bind loops near top with tight collar, arrow. Under first loops make three others, H, in front of basket, starting each just below edge of lid when in place, and forming loops downward large enough for rod, J; tie ends of loops on inside of basket. To fasten lid down, slip upper loops, I, over lower loops, H, and run a rod through, J, to lock loops together.

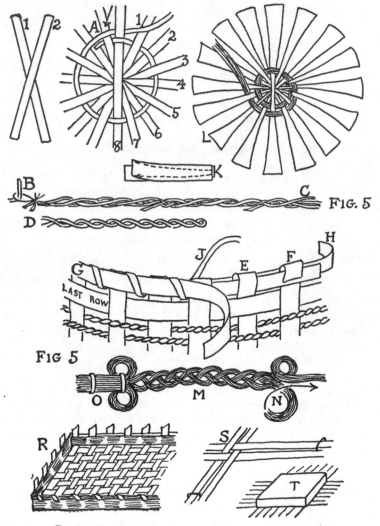

FIGURE 61—COMBINING GRASSES WITH SPLINTS

A favorite way of making grass baskets is to weave with grass ropes or braids over flat splint spokes, often dyed bright colors.

Making Grass Ropes and Braids, Figure 61—Grasses are twisted into ropes or braided to use in wicker-work baskets. To make a rope, soak grasses fifteen minutes; tie several long strands to a hook, B; twist round and round adding new strands for length desired. When twisted line kinks up into little knots, double ends C over ends B, hold ends together; a tight rope will twist in opposite direction, D. To make a braid, tie three strands or groups of strands to a hook and braid closely together. (See Fig. 69, 1.)

Covered Work Basket of Splints and Sweet Grass, Figure 61-A—Base—Cut eight ½ inch spokes 12 inches long; form radiating center, A, 5 inches across, (See Figure 34, A). *Sides*—Soak spokes, bend upward, cut out one spoke to make uneven number; weave twice around with single splint weaver. Change to grass rope weave in-and-out for 2 inches. At top weave two rows with ¼ inch splint; cover slips down easily over this flat weaving. *Border*—Bend spokes over last row, E, F. Lay ¼ inch splint around outside of top, G, and another around inside, H; bind to top row with narrow splint weaver, J. *Cover*—Cut eight 10 inch splints, soak well, fold double, as at K, cut along dotted lines to make narrow centers for a close start, as at L. Weave with unbraided grass strands to a diameter of 3 inches; use grass rope for rest of top and several rows over edge. Weave last row with ¼ inch splint; bind edge like basket using a clump of grass strands in place of outside splint, G. *Handle*—Cut some 10 inch strands; form a 3 inch braid at center, M. Leave 3 inches at ends for loops, divide into two groups, twist, as at N. Fasten handle to cover wth strong strands, O.

Square Splint Tray, Figure 61, R—Weave splints over a board, tacking first two down with spraddle tacks, S, and making plaited base, Figure 33, A. Bend spokes up over block, T; split one spoke to make uneven number; weave sides with unbraided grass. Make border as at F. This basket makes a most useful desk tray.

FIGURE 61-A—HANDY BASKET WITH SPLINT SPOKES AND TWISTED
GRASS WEAVERS

GRASS MATS

Mats of grass bundles are durable, of soft pleasing texture and beautiful color. The material is so plentiful we should find inspiration for creating many useful articles—circular mats to place under flower pots, hot plate mats, porch mats, and small rugs. Mats are made in three ways: first, by laying bundles of grasses in parallel rows and binding them together with twining stitches or rows of coiling stitches, like cat-tail mats, Figure 62, D-U; second, by making grass braids or ropes and sewing them into circles, ovals, or squares, as in corn shuck mats, Figures 66, 68; third, by plaiting crushed stems into mats and finishing their edges with a coil of fibers bound with bright colored raffia, Figure 62, A. Grasses may also be woven on a loom into effective little table runners and rugs. Use a carpet warp, and lay in several strands at a time; overlapping their ends; keep them in a wet towel.

RUSHES AND REEDS

These are used, like grasses, as bundle material in coiled basketry, or when crushed flat or split into strips, for plaiting. The surfaces of some provide strips of maroon and brown; the soft green stems of others make beautiful color backgrounds for baskets and mats—

> *"Bulrushes and reeds of such deep green,*
> *As soothed the dazzled eye with sober sheen."*
> —SHELLEY

CHAPTER XX

BASKETS OF LEAVES AND FERNS

"There's never a leaf nor a blade too mean
To be some happy creature's palace."
—LOWELL

IBROUS leaves that do not crumble when dry are used for basket making. They may be cut into strips or folded lengthwise to use for plaited baskets; or cut into even widths and crushed in the palm to use as soft weaving material over spokes; and bundles of leaves are useful for foundation material in coiled baskets, because of their lovely, deep colors and softness of texture. Both leaves and ferns are stripped of their green, leaving veins and stems to use for sewing or overlay strands.

CAT-TAILS

Cat-tail leaves, long, tough and soft green, are used in four ways: First, a single leaf makes a strong flat weaver over-spokes. Second, being of the right width they are used for plaited baskets. Third, for coiled baskets several leaves make a good bundle; for fine work the leaves are split into strips. Fourth, they make strong braids to sew into mats or market bags. Finer braids of split cat-tails may be sewed in sandal shape with two braids crossing over the toe. See cat-tail sandals and baskets, Figure 27, Nos. 5, 6, 7, 11, and 13. Gather the leaves in summer or fall; dry in the shade and store in a dry place. Cat-tail heads are gilded to make basket ornaments.

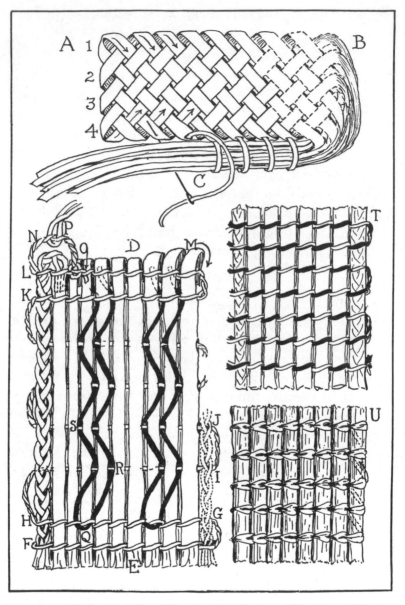

FIGURE 62—MATS OF CAT-TAILS OR RUSHES ARE DURABLE, SOFT TO
THE FEET AND OF A NATURAL TAN COLOR, MOST DESIRABLE FOR
SUMMER COTTAGES AND PORCHES

Plaited Mat, A—This plaited mat with coiled edge suggests a new way of starting a basket. Fold four long cat-tails or rush stems at their centers; place loops side by side, 1, 2, 3, 4; turn Nos. 1 and 4 sharply at corners. Plait the strands in-and-out, turning them back into weaving at edges, arrows. At end of mat, B, join strands in a coil, fasten to center with simple coiling stitches, C. Continue coiling for a mat as large as desired.

Mat With Zig-zag Design, D—This lovely mat pattern with black zig-zag design of dyed cat-tails, is made by threading single cat-tails over a rope of cat-tail fibers. First decide upon width of mat, D to E; make two braids this length for each end, F-L; cut cat-tails this length and lay parallel. (Only half a mat is shown.) Loop sewing strand around braid at corner F; twine toward right. At end of row twist upward 2 inches to G and twine left. At end of second row, H, twist upward 3 inches. For third row make holes through cat-tails with an awl; run strands through to I; twist upward 3 inches to J, repeat row I. Make rows 3 inches apart, to twining row K like H, and row L like F.

To make a bag, finish top edges of two mats as at M, fastening the looped-over ends in the twining. At end of last row L, twist weavers into loop N, fasten at O. Make similar loop on other mat; join loops at base of handle, P. Join two mats at base and sides.

To make zig-zag pattern, loop strand double through twined row, Q; carry ends upward, each across a cat-tail to R; pass under sewing strand; then upward to left, under strand at S. Repeat zig-zag pattern to row K; fasten ends on wrong side.

Twined Mat, T—This mat is of single cat-tails or rushes, or braids of soft fibers, fastened together in parallel rows with Twining. Use color in weavers or parallel strands.

Mat With Split Stitching, U—Split stitches make ornamental mats. Stitch over first row; reverse; lay second row parallel and attach, splitting first stitches; reverse, etc.

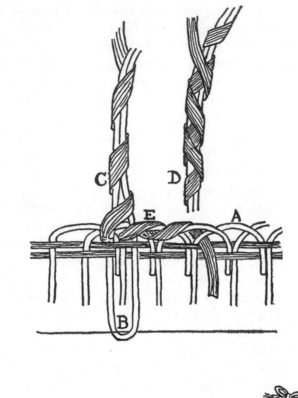

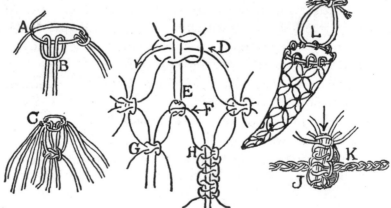

Figure 63—*Above,* LEAVES USED FOR ORNAMENTING. *Below,* TIED
BASKET OVER A HORN

[130]

LEAVES USED FOR ORNAMENTING—Figure 63

Leaves are effective when woven into bands across the surfaces of baskets or when used for ornamenting borders and handles. An open border, upper diagram, A, is wrapped round and round with green yucca or cat-tail leaves or rushes. The handle is made of a long vine looped double, B. It is wrapped with leaves, first coiling in one direction across handle, as at C, then back in opposite direction, D. Piecing is done between the handle rods.

KNOT-TYING WITH CAT-TAILS, RUSHES AND GRASSES
—Figure 63

Meshwork baskets are made by tying flexible, fibrous strands into knots, sometimes over glass jars to form vases; again with no solid background, to make basket-bags. The knot used is King Solomon's Knot, Figures 63 and 22. Use cat-tails split into strips, tough grass-stems or rushes; soak well before tying.

Tied Basket Over a Horn, Figure 63, below—Work downward from tip of horn. Make ring of a stem, A. Fold a strand double and attach its loop to ring, B. Attach eight strands, then pull two ends of ring taut and tie, C. With the four ends of two strands make a knot, tying two outer strands in a square knot over two inner ones, see G. Tie four knots around first row. Make second row ¾ inches below first, using tying strands of first row to be tied over, Figure 22. Continue with other rows, the knots in each row coming between those of preceding row. As horn widens add new strands, as at D, through middle of knot; use middle strand of this knot, E, for lower knot with another new strand added, F.

To make loops, J, to pass handle through, use two outer strands of each knot in last row to tie six complete knots, one below the other, H; turn this column of knots over in loop, J, and fasten as at K, arrow. Run hanging cord through.

A Flexible Knotted Bag—Is started as at A, B, and C. Keep inserting strands to enlarge number of knots so rows will expand outward in a radiating circle, working with the bag flat on a table. When it measures 10 inches across, lessen number of knots by cutting out strands and making fewer knots with those left, bringing bag to a smaller diameter at top. When it measures 6 to 8 inches across, make rope loops, J, and run a braid through to shirr up bag.

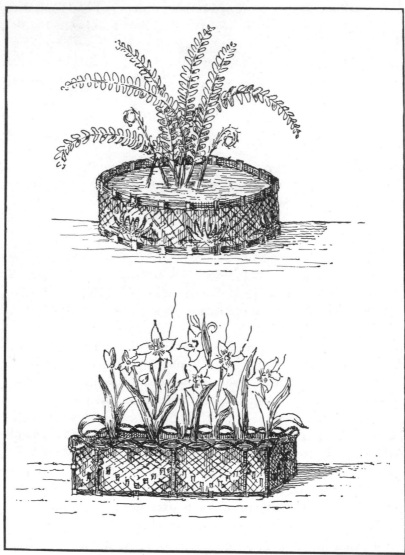

FIGURE 64—*Above*, COVERING FOR A PLANT RECEPTACLE, OF PLAITED GRASSES WITH TRIMMING OF RAFFIA. *Below*, BREAD TIN COVERED WITH MATTING, BORDER OF LOOPED GRASSES

CHAPTER XXI

FLOWER-POT CUFFS OF BRAIDED AND WOVEN STRANDS

"In all places, then, and in all seasons,
Flowers expand their light and soul-like wings,
Teaching us, by most persuasive reasons,
How akin they are to human things."
—LONGFELLOW

THE real fun of basketry lies in creating something new. Baskets we love and must have, but it is an added joy to make baskets that are new and useful for the home. These flower-pot covers were made by braiding and sewing grasses, rushes or cat-tails into small mats, then rolling them into cylindrical form, and sewing the two ends together to make basket cuffs. The idea grew from a need to procure more flower pots for sunny windows. Many of us enjoy having such a quantity and variety of flowers, it is difficult to find attractive containers for them all. Flowers are more responsive than anything, perhaps, to the thoughtful touch. The slightest care transforms them into double their loveliness, which nevertheless may be ruined if they are allowed to grow in ugly receptacles. Besides the many interesting ways that the author has discovered of making basket holders for these "smiles of the Great Spirit," as the Indian calls them, the reader will find many more that suggest themselves as natural combinations of the soft-toned materials found in the woods and fields.

One of the best colors for flower-pot covers or plant baskets is natural tan, the quiet dry-grass color which nature spreads over hill and dale in the autumn when she is painting the trees fire and gold. How vividly these stand out against the soft dead grasses of the meadows! And this same color, tan, will form a beautiful background for bright window blossoms. There is a peculiar appropriateness in giving to the surroundings of our house plants a touch of the out-of-doors—a fitness in bringing to them the same vernal backgrounds that would be theirs were they growing uncultivated in Nature's domain. The thought of rough brown vines twined over willow rods for porch boxes; bundles of weather-tinged grasses coiled into tall graceful flower cuffs; or strips of russet cedar bark plaited into basket jars for rich green foliage impels one to seek out vine-clad walls, sunlit fields sprinkled with clumps of grasses, or a stream fringed with rushes, for a handful of wild basketry materials.

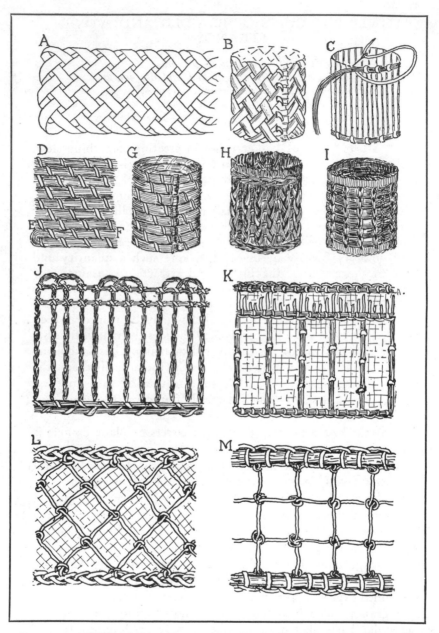

FIGURE 65—FLOWER-POT CUFFS OF PLAITED, BRAIDED OR WOVEN MATS

FLOWER-POT CUFFS—Figure 65, A to I

Mats may be rolled into round covers to slip over unattractive flower containers. These cuffs may cover both flower pot and saucer. A cuff for a medium flower pot measures 5 or 6 inches in diameter and 6 or 7 inches high.

Plaited Cuff, A, B—Measure container—height and width—and make mat 1 inch longer than distance around it and 1 inch wider than height. Plait strands, A, to this size; roll mat around container so as to fit loosely; sew ends together, B. Loose fiber ends may be hidden inside or left outside as fringe.

Cat-tail Cuff, C—Bind cat-tails together in a mat like Figure 62, D; roll mat into a cylinder, sew ends together and stitch bundles of grasses to top and bottom rims of cuff.

Grass Cuff With Coiling Stitch, D-G—Sew grasses together in horizontal rows with coiling stitch. They may be carried back and forth from row to row, E, or each row started new, F. Make mat 1½ inches longer than circumference of container to overlap ends well; soak well before rolling. This cuff may also be made in a continuous upward spiral coil.

Braided Cuff, H—Make a long braid of cat-tails or grasses, cut it into lengths, sew together in vertical rows; sew first and last strips together to make cylinder. Trim cuff with braids around top and bottom.

Cuff With Split Stitching, I—Make flat mat with split stitches, Figure 62, and roll into a cuff; or make spiral rows of a continuous grass bundle. Bind top and bottom with buttonhole stitches.

PLAIN CUFFS WITH GRASS TRIMMINGS—J to M

Grass matting or cardboard may be rolled into cylinders with or without bases and trimmed with bundles of grasses. Cardboard covered with brown paper makes a pleasing background for grasses. Paste smooth, heavy, brown paper flat over cardboard cuff; let dry, then shellac.

Braided Grasses in Loops, J—Sew vertical braids to a cardboard cuff; make loops at top; fasten horizontal bundles with crosses.

Matting Cuff Trimmed With Buttonholing, K—Trim a matting cuff with bundles of grasses; cover edges with buttonholing.

Tied Rushes Over Matting, L—Make cuff of matting; fasten cat-tail braids around top and bottom; tie raffia knots diagonally between them, first laying raffia across in one direction, then in opposite direction making knots at intersections.

Knotted Cuff with Buttonholed Edges, M—Cover cardboard cuff with brown paper; fasten a cat-tail leaf around top and bottom with buttonholing; lay strands of raffia vertically between edges, cross them with horizontal strands, knot them at intersections.

PART IV—NOVELTY BASKETS

Chapter XXII

AN OLD CRAFT FROM DIXIE

"Heap high the farmer's wintry hoard!
Heap high the golden corn!
No richer gift has Autumn poured
From out her lavish horn!"
—*The Corn Song*—Whittier

WHO would ever dream that out of the corn husk one could make fancy hats and bags and other novelties of a texture resembling expensive straw? The list is a long one, comprising baskets of interesting form—doily sets, mats, whisk broom holders, wall racks, rugs, hearth brooms and many other unique things. The craft originated in the south where Dixie folk observed the clever ways in which negroes sewed husks together to make mats and brushes. The art is simple enough to tempt unskilled fingers. One just braids the strips of corn husks then sews the braids together in any fancied shape.

GATHERING CORN HUSKS

Corn husks may be gathered any time after the green of the leaves has turned to tan—in late fall when the corn has been shocked, or even after it has been gathered. Moisture causes the husks to deteriorate, so those kept dry under barn roofs are the best. Lay them in a dry place to keep them from molding.

PREPARING THEM FOR USE

Corn husks are fibrous and strong. It is impossible to tear a leaf crosswise. Field corn gives the best colored and strongest husks. Sweet corn is paler and not as durable. Tear off the outer coarse grained leaves from the ear and use the soft textured creamy ones within. These are finer fibered, more pliable and take dye better. After sorting these out cut off their thick ends with scissors. A bushel of leaves will make a good sized rug.

DYEING CORN HUSKS

Corn husks, especially the inner creamy leaves, take dye beautifully; but no dyed shade can equal the natural color of the husk which is often used unaltered. For dyeing cut off the thick ends. First wet the leaves fifteen minutes in warm water. Use ordinary cloth dyes, following the directions given on the packages, but using twice the amount of dye directed for a pound because the husks absorb color readily. After boiling let the husks stand twelve hours in the dye. Then rinse off once in cold water. Let them dry, away from the sun. Keep them in a dry place until ready for use.

In the same pan of dye always dye the thread or raffia to be used for sewing them together; but remove directly after boiling. If the thread seems to be absorbing too much color remove from the boiling liquid before taking out the husks. Deep rich dyes will give the leaves exquisite tones—brown, green, purple, red, black and blue. Orange and yellow give a successful dye, but the color will not contrast well with the natural colored husk, whereas the darker colors make stunning borders and designs against the natural background.

PAINTING AND STENCILING

Oil paints or hat dyes may be used to paint designs or borders on finished articles of the undyed husks. A stencil helps in getting a series of uniform motifs. Stripes following the course of the braids as they go around an oval or a circle are effective, and square mats may be decorated with broad bands or borders.

FIVE WAYS TO USE CORN HUSKS

Corn husks may be put together in five different ways. First they may be braided and the braids sewed into circular or square form, Figure 66. Second, they may be folded into little pointed pieces and these stitched down on buckram or cardboard to make hats or baskets, Figure 67. Third, they may be rolled into continuous strands and bound with raffia into mats, rugs and trays, Figure 68. Fourth, they may be woven on a loom into table mats and strips for various purposes, Figure 68. Lastly, they may be tied and bound into groups to make hearth brooms and floor mops, Figure 68.

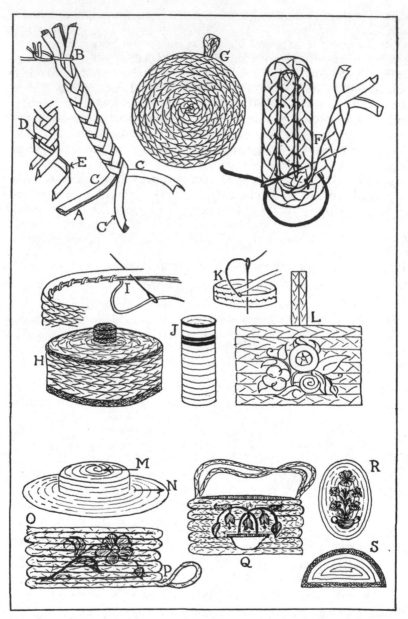

FIGURE 66—BRAIDED CORN HUSKS. *Below*, GARDEN SET OF HAT, MAT
AND BAG

1. BRAIDED CORN HUSKS—Figure 66

Braided corn husks make wide hats, bags, mats, rugs, sets of table doilies and baskets. The braids may be of any width: wide braids are best for rugs and baskets as they work up quickly; narrow braids are effective for table mats and hats. For a wide rug-braid, cut the husks into 1 inch strips; fold these double, making each strand ½ inch wide, the finished braid, 1 inch wide. For a braid ¾ inch wide, cut strands ¾ inch wide and fold double. For a braid ⅝ inch wide cut strips ⅝ inch wide and fold. Still narrower braids make fine baskets and table mats.

Soak strips in warm water before braiding. Fold three strips double, as at A, tie ends tightly to a hook with cord, B, braid so folded edges lie uppermost or away from worker, C. Crease each strip neatly at side and fold over for next strip. To piece strips fold a new strip, push its end under old one, as at D, and conceal new end by turning old strip over it, at side of braid; at next turn, E, bend new strip over old end. Sew into an oval, F, or circle, G.

BRAIDED BAGS AND BASKETS

To make basket, H, sew braid around in a circle to form base; coil upwards for sides. Make lid like pine needle work-basket lid, Figure 57, J, starting knob with fine braid. Make ledge inside basket for lid to rest on, I, sewing roll of husks around, ¼ inch from top. A tall jar cover, J, is made with a long braid coiled upward. The arm basket at L is made of a cylinder of braids, K, crushed flat and sewed together at base. Attach braided handle.

GARDEN SET OF CORN HUSKS

This garden set of hat, mat and bag are convenient for long hours of gardening. Over the arm goes the bag to hold trowel and scissors, over the wrist goes the handle of the mat to kneel on, and over all, lending its grateful shade is the corn husk hat. Start hat at crown, M, sew braid around in circle 7 or 8 inches across, then downward and outward, as at N. For the mat, sew braids back and forth as at O; form loop, P, at one corner; make mat at least 18 x 12 inches. Make bag at Q like mat but twice as deep; fold double at base; sew sides together with raffia; attach handles. A round garden mat is shown at G.

BRAIDED RUGS AND MATS

Corn husk rugs are durable yet soft under foot; their texture and color are attractive; they make excellent porch rugs or bathroom mats, washed clean by brushing with soap suds and warm water. Make rugs round as at G; oval as at F and R; oblong or square as at O; and half round as at S. Two half-round rugs make one large round one.

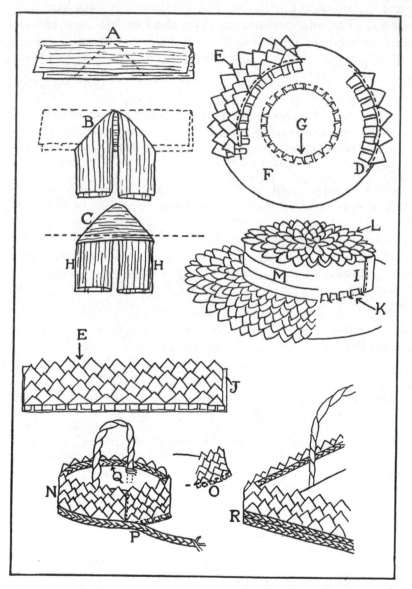

FIGURE 67—ARTICLES MADE OF CORN HUSKS FOLDED INTO POINTS

2. CORN HUSKS FOLDED INTO POINTS—Figure 67

Corn husks may be cut into little strips, folded into points and sewed to firm cloth foundations to make decorative hats, bags, and baskets. The soft inner leaves, either dyed or left their natural color, are used for the points.

Each point is made of a piece of husk cut 3 inches long and from 1½ to 2 inches wide. Fold it double lengthwise, A; fold ends down at center, B; sew down on right side, dotted lines, C, between point and tabs, H. Stitch points in rows on buckram foundation, D, each point overlapping preceding one slightly. Points of second row, E, should come between those of first row, etc. Machine stitching is best.

The husk hat, 15 inches in diameter, is made on a buckram or cardboard base, F, cut with an opening at center, G, to allow for crown. Cut circle a little smaller than head size, slit up into tabs as at G. Start sewing points to outside rim, D; in last row tabs should cover buckram tabs, G. For sides cut length of buckram, I, to go around head; cover with husk points, J; sew ends together, I, sew cylinder outside of tabs, K. Make top of hat, L, on circle of buckram. Start sewing points around outer edge and come toward center. Sew crown to sides. Line brim of hat with chintz.

To make baskets like N, cover a cardboard strip with points, J, sew into a cylinder, N, and sew this to plain cardboard bottom, O. Make handle of a roll or braid of husks over wire; sew down to inside of basket. Line basket with chintz. Cover outside of bottom edge P, and inside of top edge, Q, with braids. Square baskets are made around a square base in the same way, as at R. Any number of braids, sometimes of dyed husks, may be sewed around the edge.

3. CORN HUSKS ROLLED AND SEWED—Figure 68

Rolled husks may be sewed with raffia or twine into trays, baskets, rugs and seat mats. Rolled husks make strong useful articles resembling expensive things made of rush.

Prepare husks by cutting off the thick ends and soaking in water. Use leaves entire but carefully trim off any rough edges. To make roll, use three leaves, roll two of them inside a third, rolling from edge to edge like a cigarette, as in Figure 68.

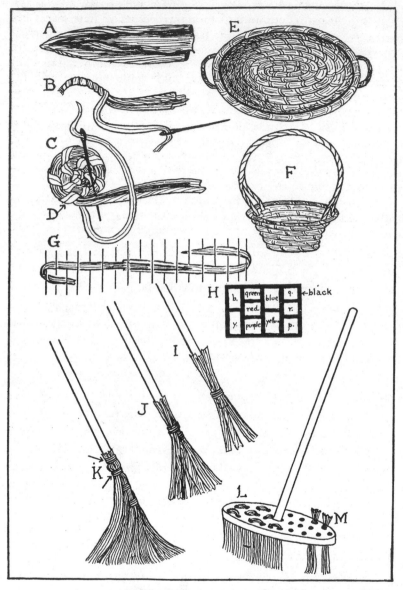

FIGURE 68—*Above*, CORN HUSKS ROLLED AND SEWED. *Center*, WOVEN HUSKS. *Below*, CORN HUSK HEARTH BROOMS AND MOPS

Start a basket or mat center by wrapping the narrow end of a husk roll, Figure 68, A, with raffia, B. Sew into circle, C, with simple stitches around roll, D. Use pine needle basketry stitches, Figure 56. Piece roll frequently, slipping points of new pieces between new and old rows. Inside husks of roll need not be perfect as they do not show. In finishing off last row, taper roll gradually to a point; also in changing from one color to another, taper off last row of old color, and start new color with a narrw roll, increasing it gradually.

Rugs made from thick rolls of husks are heavy, flat and soft. Dye some husks a deep color for several rows of border, or paint or stencil a simple pattern on rug when finished and dry. Seat mats of rolled husks made like rugs are strong and useful for kitchen or porch. To make rugs lie flat, wet them when finished, and weight down with heavy boards until dry.

Attractive trays of rolled husks are made with a low border and handles, as at E. Almost any kind of basket may be formed with them. The circular basket at F has wire handles wound with raffia. Make sewing baskets, scrap baskets and flower bowls by sewing rolled husks around in coils.

4. WOVEN CORN HUSKS—Figure 68, G

Narrow runners, rugs, table mats and strips for bags may be woven of corn husks on a loom, using a cotton warp of the same or a harmonious color. The result is a grass fabric like matting. To weave the husks, trim off the thick ends; soak in water; keep in a damp towel. Tear each leaf into strips ½ inch wide; lay strips along through warp shed, laying point of each on top of wider end of last one; fold husks to turn from row to row as at G. Dyed husks make bright borders. Tie cotton warp into a fringe.

5. HEARTH BROOMS AND MOPS—Figure 68, K, M

Use the tougher corn husks for brooms and mops.

To make a hearth broom, cut stick ¾ inch in diameter, 2½ feet long; brush with brown stain; 6 inches from top paint series of checks or stripes, pattern H. For brush part dye husks one of border colors; string ten husks on a cord at their centers and tie them around a notch made near base of stick, as at I; wrap tightly over string with wire. Tie second group, J, ¾ inch above first one in same way; also third group, K. Bind last bundle twice at top with wire. Trim ends of husks even.

The board of mop, L, is ¾ inch thick, bored with ⅜ inch holes. Bore large handle hole diagonally; insert handle and glue. Slip as many husks as possible through holes, using a wire hook or hairpin to pull them up and down. As they absorb water they swell and fit snugly. Husks may be inserted straight, as at M.

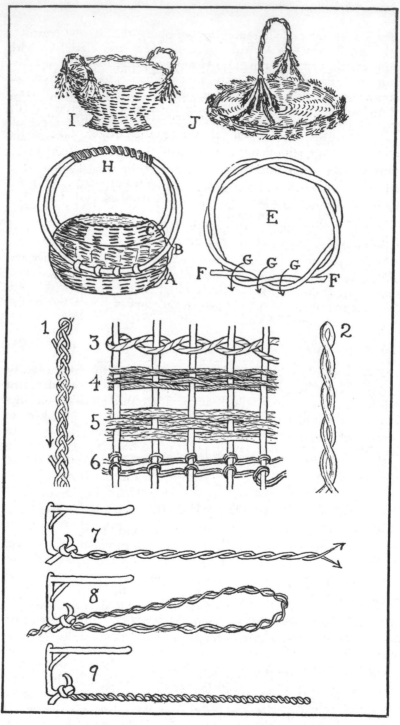

Figure 69—*Above*, H, ROUND NUT BASKET WITH HANDLES; I, BOWL WITH GRASS TASSELS; J, FLAT BON-BON TRAY. *Below*, METHODS OF WEAVING MINIATURE BASKETS

CHAPTER XXIII

MINIATURE BASKETS—FIGURE 69

*O*OR learning basketry, miniature baskets serve as excellent practise models. Little material is required and the quick satisfaction of seeing the basket take shape rapidly, at once stimulates and rewards the effort. Red clover, timothy, redtop, even the stalks of ferns may be woven into dainty baskets. Soft green and tan grasses weave delicate tones between fine ivory colored spokes. Grass heads may be left for ornament, and colorful autumn berries, little bunches of acorns, even groups of hard buds from the end of a branch, all give charm to small baskets.

Once completed miniature baskets make attractive dinner party favors, gifts, etc. As containers for candies and nuts they are better than the usual paper affairs, for they can be kept, and put to future use in various ways—to hold jewelry or cuff buttons, matches, pins, etc.

Methods of Weaving Used, Figure 69, 1-9—A braid of grasses is shown at 1, a roll at 2. Both braided and rolled grasses are used in Pairing Weave, 3; Simple Weave, 4; Double Under-and-Over Weave, 5; Wraping Stitch, 6; Double Pairing, Figure 8; and Japanese Weave, Figure 7. The spokes are fine or split rods.

Round Nut Basket With Handles, A-H—Cut eight spokes of No. 2, 10 inches long; weave Simple Base, Figure 3, 2 inches across. Weave sides in two weaves, several rounds of Pairing, A; Double Weave, B; Pairing, C. For handles make two circles of fine reed, splice ends, cover splicing with wrapping, H. At E is a twisted handle circle made of fine reed 24 inches long, ends, F, overlapping, and fastening stitches, G, taken across overlapped ends.

Bowl With Grass Tassels, I—This little bowl is woven with grasses over fine spokes. Its central shape is similar to A; an added base support is made by inserting extra spokes into weaving at narrow base groove. Handles are bundles of grasses wrapped with raffia.

Flat Bon-bon Tray, J—This basket for small cakes or candies has a Sixteen-spoke Base, Figure 4, with fine split willow spokes, and weavers of rolled grasses. The handle has forks at each side made of hat wire twisted with grasses, their tassels left showing.

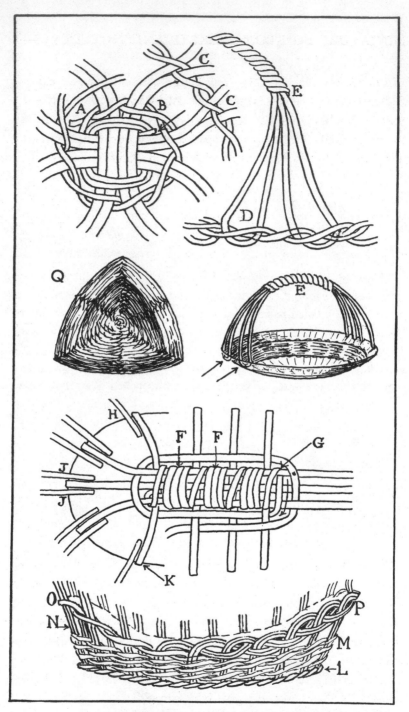

Figure 70—MINIATURE BON-BON BASKETS AND NUT TRAYS. E, LITTLE
CANDY BASKET; O, SMALL NUT TRAY; Q, THREE-SIDED COILED BASKET

Little Candy Basket, A-E—This round basket for a tiny cake or candied fruit is a clever party favor. Make base with eight No. 2 spokes 12 inches long; add second weaver for Pairing, A, continue around pairs, B, for five rows; separate spokes into single ones, C; gradually curve base upward in a basin shape 3 inches across. Finish with Closed Border No. 2. For handle cut two No. 2 reeds 18 inches long, fold double, insert loops around border, D; carry strands over to opposite side and conceal ends in weaving; join four strands at top with raffia wrapping, E. A pretty way to make this basket is to weave with two different materials, a center of one, a band of the other and a top section of the first.

Small Nut Tray, O—One of the prettiest of dinner gifts is a small tray for nuts made exactly like a large one. It may be stained in a wood color or dyed a bright tint. Make an oval base like that at Figure 5, L, with three long spokes of No. 3, 4 inches long, and four short spokes 3 inches long; wrap in between spokes as shown here at F, and start weaving around oval, as at G. Make oval base 3 x 2 inches. For sides cut twenty spokes of No. 2, 5 inches long, insert one beside each short spoke, H, two at each long spoke, J; clip base spokes level against weaving, K. Weave a round of Double Pairing at edge of base, L. For sides use Pairing Weave around spokes, M. To make a close border insert extra spokes, N; weave final round of Pairing over pairs of spokes lifting it above other weaving at each end of tray, O, P, this raised part taking place of handles. Make Rapid Braid Border, Figure 15.

Three-sided Coiled Basket—Basket favors made with coiled grasses are delicate. This little token is made of small bundles of grasses of delicate soft texture, sewed together with coiling stitch or with a decorative pine needle stitch, Figure 56. Start base with a tiny coil, Figure 46. After several rows gradually shape edges into a triangle. Make diameter of base 2 or 3 inches, then roll sides gently outward and upward, and when near top, slightly inward. Shellac basket to give it a soft gloss.

FIGURE 71—BASKET BIRD NESTS

Above, Cane and corn husk birdhouse. *Below, left,* Birdhouse of unpeeled coral-berry vines. *Below, right,* Wren nest of honeysuckle vines, trimmed with yucca leaves

[148]

CHAPTER XXIV

BASKET BIRD NESTS

"The little bird sits at his door in the sun,
A-tilt like a blossom among the leaves,
And lets his illumined being o'er-run
With the deluge of summer it receives."
—LOWELL

ONE wonders if our bird neighbors, who so practically set up housekeeping in boxes, painted tin cans and hollow sections of limbs, might not actually prefer an attractive little home of basket form, woven more like their own work, of wild vines and grasses. The best materials to use are unpeeled honeysuckle, coral-berry, or other flexible vines; splints of oak, ash or maple; unpeeled willow rods; split spruce roots; and cane, cat-tails or rush. For trimmings and water-sheds use such soft leafy materials as yucca leaves, fern stems, clumps of pine needles, raffia and corn husks, either natural or dyed green or brown. Even soft bits of down may be worked into the weaving, thus attracting the bird to a nest supplied with building material; for birds do come where they find thoughtful provision for them.

BIRD REQUIREMENTS

Before making our basket bird nest we must know the habits of the birds to occupy it. The basket must be wide enough to accommodate their tail feathers and deep enough to suit their fancy, for birds have preferences. Most important of all is the size of the opening, for some birds seem to want to be able just to squeeze through the hole: wrens, chickadees, purple martins, bluebirds and great crested flycatchers. A larger hole might admit enemies. Others, like robins, barn swallows and song sparrows, do not confine themselves in houses but prefer open nests or shelters. The entrance hole should face south and the house tip forward so rain will not enter the hole.

To help the bird-nest builder in making a successful home for his particular bird friends, the following guide is copied from Farmer' Bulletin, No. 1456, HOMES FOR BIRDS, issued by the U. S. Department of Agriculture.

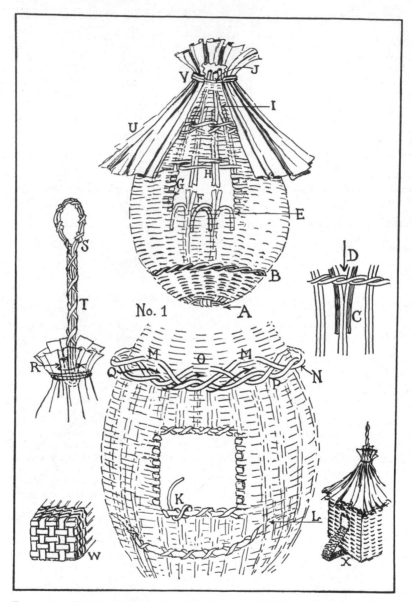

FIGURE 72—DIAGRAMS OF CANE AND CORN HUSK HOUSE FOR BLUEBIRDS

DIMENSIONS FOR BIRD NESTS

SPECIES	Floor of cavity	Depth of cavity	Entrance above floor	Diameter of entrance	Height above ground
	Inches	Inches	Inches	Inches	Feet
Bluebirds	5 × 5	8	6	1½	5-10
Robin	6 × 8	8	(¹)	(¹)	6-15
Chickadees	4 × 4	8-10	6- 8	1⅛	6-15
Titmice	4 × 4	8-10	6- 8	1¼	6-15
Nuthatches	4 × 4	8-10	6- 8	1¼	12-20
House wren	4 × 4	6- 8	1- 6	1	6-10
Carolina wren	4 × 4	6- 8	1- 6	1⅛	6-10
Tree swallow	5 × 5	6	1- 5	1½	10-15
Barn swallow	6 × 6	6	(¹)	(¹)	8-12
Purple martin	6 × 6	6	1	2½	15-20
Song sparrow	6 × 6	6	(²)	(²)	1- 3
House finch	6 × 6	6	4	2	8-12
Phoebe	6 × 6	6	(¹)	(¹)	8-12
Crested flycatcher	6 × 6	6-10	6- 8	2	8-20
Flicker	7 × 7	16-18	14-16	2½	6-20
Red-headed woodpecker ...	6 × 6	12-15	9-12	2	12-20
Downy woodpecker	4 × 4	8-10	6- 8	1¼	6-20
Hairy woodpecker	6 × 6	12-15	9-12	1½	12-20

¹ One or more sides open.   ² All sides open.

CANE AND CORN HUSK BIRDHOUSE—Figure 72, No. 1

This straw colored birdhouse, photo in Figure 71, is made of narrow cane or splint weavers over round spokes, with a tufted water-shed of corn husks. The dimensions are for a bluebird.

Base and Sides—Start at A with sixteen spokes 2 feet long, size No. 3. Weave Indian Center, Figure 4, with a single strand over pairs of spokes up to B, 3 inches from start, diameter at B, 5 or 6 inches. At this point insert a pair of spokes at each pair but one, shaded spokes, C. Separate groups of four into pairs, as at D, weave once around twenty-five pairs with No. 3 in Triple Coil. Weave in-and-out 3 inches up to opening, E. *Opening*—Cut off one or two pairs 1 inch above weaving, F, turn down into weaving; weave back and forth at each side, G, taking extra turns around spokes at edges. When opening is 1½ inches high insert pairs, H, to replace cut-out spokes; weave 1 inch above opening, cut out one spoke of each pair, join adjacent single spokes in new pairs, I. Weave 1 inch to top; bind spokes with wire, J. Wrap edges of opening, as at K. *Perch*—Make perch, L, ½ inch below opening, of a No. 6 rod, 12 inches long, whittled at ends, inserted into weaving at each side, L, and wrapped with crosses. *Bridge*—Make roof-extension N, for birds to land on, of a single No. 3 strand. Fasten end ¾ inch above opening, carry it around basket; insert it under spokes every 2 inches, M, forming loops, N, extending 1 inch out from basket. Loop around basket a second time, inserting at points O, midway between points M. Go around a third time, twisting strand around outer edge only, P, and a fourth time twisting along grooves of last round, arrows, Q. *Handle*—Insert two pieces of No. 3 reed through wire at top of house, R, carry upward 1½ feet, make loop S, carry down to start of wire. Coil cane upward around handle in one direction, downward in opposite direction, forming crosses, T.

Watershed—Tie corn husks U, 7 or 8 inches long, in a clump around wire-bound top, as at V; bind with wire.

A square birdhouse of flat weavers is shown at X, with square plaited base at W. Make a slanting perch by bending unused spokes at opening down into the shape shown at X and weaving under and over them with cane.

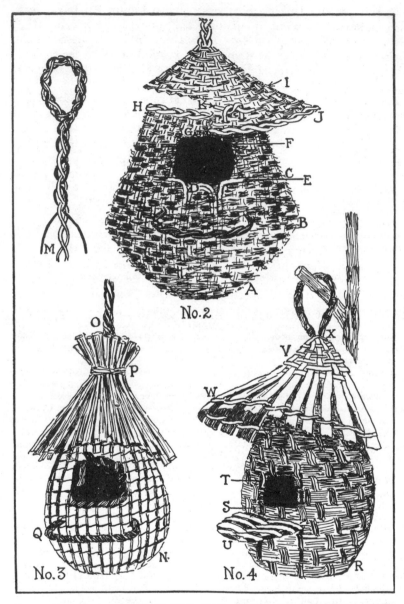

FIGURE 73—*Above,* DIAGRAM FOR BIRD HOUSE OF UNPEELED VINES.
Below, left, SMALL BIRD NEST OF SPLINTS AND RUSHES. *Below, right,*
TREE SWALLOW'S NEST OF SPLINTS AND GRASSES

BIRDHOUSE OF UNPEELED VINES—FIGURE 73, No. 2

In this woodsy looking birdhouse, photo Figure 71, lower left, both spokes and weavers are of unpeeled honeysuckle or other flexible vines: spokes, size No. 4 or 5; weavers, No. 3 or 4. Scraggly knobs and knots along the stems give a rustic beauty to the basket-nest. The roof is detachable so as to clean the house out between seasons.

Base—Weave Indian Basket Base, Figure 4, with sixteen spokes 20 inches long and a seventeenth half pair. The slope from A to B is 3½ inches; diameter at B, 6 inches; distance from B to C, 2 inches. *Opening*—Cut out two pairs of spokes, conceal in weaving, D, E. Weave back and forth at each side of opening, F, taking extra turns around edges to fill in gaps. Weave 1 inch above opening to H, narrowing diameter to 4 inches. At H finish with Closed Border No. 2, Figure 12. *Handle*—Follow diagram at M, directions given at Figure 19, W. *Roof*—Weave separately to extend over border. Start center like base with sixteen spokes 15 inches long, inserting seventeenth pair. Weave downward in tent shape, making slope to I, 2½ inches; diameter, 4½ inches to match that at H. Weave 2 inches farther to J, diameter, 7 to 8 inches. Finish with Rapid Braid Border, Figure 15, or separate spokes and use a closed border over single spokes, Figure 12. Tie roof down to border of birdhouse at three places, as at K. *Perch*—Make a loop of twisted vines, 3 inches across, like twisted handle, Figure 18, N.

SMALL BIRD NEST OF SPLINTS AND RUSHES—
FIGURE 73, No. 3

This little house may be woven over narrow splints of oak or ash, with rushes or grasses of a light color to match and a tufted water-shed of corn-shucks. Another combination for this unique nest is cedar bark strips of brown for spokes, rushes or raffia for rows of pairing, and green yucca leaves for water-shed and trimmings.

Base—Cut six strips of split cedar bark ¼ to ⅜ inch wide, and 14 inches long. Start them in a circular base, Figure 34, A, and weave around them with two flexible strands, using Pairing Weave. Make base 4 inches in diameter. Turn splints up gradually, weaving sides in spiral rounds ¼ inch apart, as at N. *Opening*—Make a small opening, 1 inch in diameter, 4 inches above base, by cutting off several splints and turning them over at edge of hole like top of a splint basket. Cover edges with over-and-over stitches of grasses, rushes or yucca leaves. Narrow nest above door by cutting out splints, weave to top of basket, and finally bind those left with wire at the top. *Handle*—Tie ends of several narrow splints around the wire and twist upward into a rope as at O, curve over in a loop, and twist back again upon itself, fastening all ends down with wire at top of basket. *Roof*—Tie material chosen for watershed, which should be same as trimming at edge of hole, around top of basket in a firm clump and bind with wire, then cover wire with raffia or grasses, as at P. The *Perch* is a piece of bent twig inserted into weaving below opening, and wound over with rushes, grasses or leaves, as at Q.

TREE SWALLOW NEST OF SPLINTS AND GRASSES— FIGURE 73, No. 4

A coiled house of sewed grasses or corn husks with a sloping roof of splints suggests the tree swallow, and this nest is made the right size for him or for the violet-green swallow. Almost any kind of material may be used for the foundation coil—rushes, grasses, flexible vines, etc., and the sewing strand may be of raffia or flexible vines.

Base—Start basket with a coiled center, Figure 47, and coil outward until base is 5 inches in diameter. Gradually curve upward as at R, to a height of 2 inches, as far as opening. *Opening*—This should not be more than 1½ inches in diameter. To make it, cut coil at S; carry it around in back of basket to other side of opening and cut off. To support edges of opening, make a loop of a piece of wire, shown by dark line at T, and insert down into weaving at both sides of opening so that loop of wire forms arch over opening. Fasten cut edges of row just made to this wire, then start new coils above S, tying their edges to wire, until hole is 1½ inches high. Wrap edges with grasses or raffia. At top of opening continue coiling all around basket for a distance of 3 inches, making house about 6 inches high. *Roof*—Cross eight splints, ¼ to ½ inches wide, and 9 inches long, at their centers like a circular splint base, and weave around them with a narrow splint, as at V, for a diameter of 1½ inches. Then leave splints uncovered for 1 inch or more, and bind their outer ends together with one or more rows of pairing, using a long splint folded double, as at W. The *Handle* is made of a clump of grasses twisted around a wire and bound to it with raffia. Tie one end of handle to top of basket, push other end up through center of roof, as at X, make handle loop, and bring end down through roof again, fastening ends underneath with wire. The *Perch* is made of a bent twig inserted into the coiling and interlaced with a well-soaked splint, as at U.

FIGURE 74

"*Where shall man wander and where shall he dwell,*
Beautiful birds, that ye come not as well?
Ye have nests on the mountain all rugged and stark,
Ye have nests in the forest all tangled and dark:
Ye build and ye brood 'neath the cottager's eaves,
And ye sleep on the sod 'mid the bonnie green leaves."

—WILLIAM H. THOMSON.

LIST OF NATURAL BASKETRY MATERIALS FOUND IN THE UNITED STATES

FOLLOWING is a list of plants usable as basketry material. In store for you is the delightful experience of finding still others while pioneering in your vicinity. The Indians employed sometimes the complete stem, leaf or root, again strips cut from them. Native materials are dried to give them their final shrinkage, then soaked until pliable before using. Gathering basketry supplies does not entail damage to plant life:—shoots are trimmed from shrub or tree as for pruning; grasses are cut; the one-year old vines are pulled away leaving greater room for the new growth; only old or end roots are used. To provide an adequate supply for camp or school, it is a good plan to plant an acre of basketry plants native to the region. A bed of willows, a bank covered with vines, a row of field corn, some tough grasses and rushes, and some ash, oak or maple trees planted in cycles, would furnish a satisfactory supply of round, flat and flexible materials.

VINES

Boston and English Ivy—(Cultivated and occasionally wild) Smaller woody vines used for spokes, larger ones split for fine weavers.

Clematis—(Many species native east of Rockies, some cultivated) Woody vines used whole for spokes; split, for fine weavers.

Honeysuckle—(Various cultivated species; occasionally wild) Vines peeled or unpeeled used for spokes and weavers.

Smilax—(Various species in N. America) Shoots with roughnesses removed make strong flexible basketry material.

Wisteria—(Native species Eastern and Southern States, foreign, cultivated and escaped to wild) One-year shoots, peeled or unpeeled, make spokes; finer shoots, weavers. Strip shoots of their bark by running a sharp knife down each side and carefully pulling off the sections. These green-gray bark strips make effective weaves over the white peeled vines. (See basket bird-house, Figure 27)

FLEXIBLE RUNNERS

Coralberry—(New Jersey to Georgia, Kansas, Texas, west to S. Dakota) Tough runners, peeled or unpeeled, used for spokes and weavers.

Grapevine—(Various species in N. America) Fine rootlets used for weaving; woody parts of stem and root split into narrow weaving strips.

Virginia Creeper—(Eastern half of U. S. and cultivated) Low, tough woody runners used for spokes and weavers.

FLEXIBLE SHOOTS

White Birch—(Nova Scotia to Delaware, west to Michigan) Narrow flexible twigs used as weaving material. Boil shoots to remove bark.

Calycanthus or Strawberry Shrub—(Northern states) Young used unpeeled. Frequently bark is stripped off and used as flexible ing material.

Cottonwood—(Various species widely distributed) Flexible used like willow, for spokes and weavers; rods split into three or six sections for fine weaving. Shoots also pliable enough to use as foundation material in coiled baskets. Many Indian gambling baskets have a cottonwood foundation.

Hazelnut—(Northeastern Canada to Dakota, south to Florida) Shoots used for spokes and weavers. Wood is light and popular for carrying baskets. The Hupa Indians, noted for their beautiful basketry, made their burden baskets and flat salmon plates of this material.

Mulberry—(Massachusetts to Nebraska, south to Gulf) Flexible twigs make excellent weaving material; also adapted to splitting into fine weavers like willow rods.

Poplar—(Various species widely distributed) Flexible twigs used entire for spokes or split into three segments to provide fine weavers. Young shoots make good foundation material to coil over.

Rabbit Brush—(West and Middle West) Fine branches of this shrub used as weft to make wicker placques and finely woven baskets.

Serviceberry—(Maine to Iowa, south to Gulf) Peeled branches used as stiff uprights in strong carrying baskets; also to make strong rims for basket edges bound with flexible strands.

Fragrant Three-leaf Sumac—(Vermont to Minnesota, south to Gulf) Slender branches of this low-growing species used by Indians more than any other rod-like material except willow. Rods were used peeled for warp; for weft, branch was split into three parallel strips, two outer bark-covered strips discarded, inner flat tough strand kept for weaving. Strands were blackened for use in dark patterns by soaking a week in an infusion of the berry stems of the elder. (Do not confuse this species with three-leaf poison sumac or swamp sumac.)

Syringa—(Widely cultivated) Light pithy stems used to make carrying baskets.

Willow—(Widely distributed) Shoots used as spokes and weavers; split into three or six parts for fine wicker weaving or coiling foundations.

Weeping Willow—(Cultivated and escaped to the wild, U. S. and Canada) Long delicate withes afford excellent rods for weavers, larger ones for spokes; split into three or six parts, strands are pliable enough for fine wicker weaving or coiling foundations.

FIBROUS ROOTS

Alder—(N. America) Fine roots used as weft to begin baskets.

Balm of Gilead—(Cultivated variety of balsam poplar widely distributed from Nova Scotia to Minnesota and north and westward) Roots used for weaving heavy bases and lower basket sides.

Bracken—(Throughout U. S.) Rootstock split into two flat strips of hard-celled tissue useful in making dark patterns.

Cedar—(Throughout U. S.) Split roots, strong and fibrous, used to make water-tight baskets with close twining or wrapping.

Elm—(Newfoundland to Florida, west to Rockies) Roots afford excellent weaving material when split into fine strips. Bundles of strips make foundation coils.

Red Fir—(Sierra Nevada range) Split roots used for fine baskets.

Hemlock—(Nova Scotia to Minnesota, south to Alabama) Split roots make strong weavers.

Horsetail or Scouring Rush—(Widely distributed) Strips of the fibrous rootstock split from its surface for weaving dark purple patterns over foundation splints of cedar root.

Black Locust—(Pennsylvania to Georgia, west to Iowa and Oklahoma) Rootlets used with yellow bark left on to give color, as rod weavers or foundation material in coiling. Larger roots split and two outer sections with bark used as weavers.

Mulberry—(Massachusetts to Nebraska, south to Gulf) Fine yellow rootlets used unpeeled for rod work or coiling; larger ones split into three parallel sections, two outer ones used as weavers.

Osage Orange—(Common hedge plant escaped to wild, widely distributed) Yellow root, split or entire, used like mulberry.

Digger Pine—(Foothills of southern California) Roots warmed in hot damp ashes, strands split off before they cool.

Sugar Pine—(Western Coast States) Roots steamed under sand with a fire above. Slender strands split from them, used as fibrous wrapping material around spokes.

Georgia or Yellow Pine—(Eastern States) Roots split into fine strips for close weaving.

Sassafras—Pale yellow root with its aromatic bark used as flexible rod material, preferably with colorful bark left on.

Sitka Spruce—(Alaska to California) Roots boiled and split to make coarse foundation splints.

Black Spruce, White Spruce and Red Spruce—(Northern U. S. and Canada) All these species have tough fibrous roots split into strong dark tan weaving material. Roots of saplings are the most available.

Yucca—(Coast from N. Carolina to Louisiana, Texas) Slender red roots used to make colored figures in fine weaves.

Willow—(Various species Newfoundland to British Columbia, south to Florida and Mexico) Roots split into fine strips, used as weft to begin baskets.

SPLIT BARKS

Basswood—(New Brunswick to Dakota, south to Gulf) Inner bark split into fibrous, flexible weaving strips.

Paper Birch—(Labrador to Alaskan coast, northern U. S.) Bark stripped into narrow flat layers used for overlay patterns.

Red Cedar—(Sierra Nevada, California, Oregon, cultivated in New York, Pennsylvania, Massachusetts) Cinnamon-red bark split into strips for making pack baskets or flat bags.

White Cedar—(Seaboard states, Maine, Mississippi) Similar to red cedar.

Hazel—(Nova Scotia to Black Hills, south to Gulf) Finer shoots peeled and used whole to make warp; larger ones split to make weaving material. Small twigs of hazel spring up from burned-over ground.

Indian Hemp or Dogbane—(Atlantic to Pacific coast) Inner bark split into fibrous, cordy lengths much used to make carrying loops for baskets and to start basket centers.

Oregon Maple—(Western N. America) White inner bark peeled in spring and split, making baskets so closely woven as to hold water.

Red Mulberry—(Massachusetts to Nebraska, south to Gulf) Bark divides into scaly plates like splints. When pounded and crushed it makes flexible basketry fibers.

White Pine—(Southern Canada and eastern states; along Alleghenies to eastern Kentucky and Tennessee) Wood may be sliced with a sharp knife into thin, flat strips useful for flat weaving or plaiting.

Redbud—(New Jersey to Missouri, south to Gulf) Wood split and used as weaving material with or without bark. Strips with bark left on used for dark red patterns. Narrow threads of wood used for fine weaving.

Sassafras—(Maine to Michigan, south to Gulf) Thick, dark, reddish-brown bark breaks into broad flat ridges used for spokes or split for weavers.

Screw Bean—(Southwest U. S.) Golden-brown inner bark of this bush split into fine strands useful in plaiting or flat weaving. They resemble raffia in appearance but are much coarser.

Black Walnut—(Massachusetts to Nebraska, south to Gulf) Split inner bark used to make black patterns.

Vine Maple—(Western N. America) Vine-like runners grow along the ground and strike root frequently. Split into dark tan-colored strands, used like strips of cane.

Yew—(Mountains of coast from Alaska to southern California) Light brown or red wood split into flexible, flat weaving material.

SPLINTS

Black Ash—(Northern and eastern Canada, south to Virginia and Arkansas) Inner bark split into smooth lengths for splints.

Elm—(Newfoundland to Florida, west to Rocky Mountains) Inner bark split for coarse basket material.

Hickory—(Maine to Florida, west to Nebraska and Texas) Yellow inner bark split into thin layers used for patterns against contrasting background. Hickory splints, being durable, of a smooth texture and pleasing color, are much used for plaited bottoms of chairs and porch furniture; also for clothes baskets and wood baskets.

White Maple; Red or Swamp Maple—(Eastern N. America) Logs allowed to soak several months in lakes or streams; splints pounded and stripped from their inner bark.

White Oak—(Maine to Minnesota, south to Gulf) Inner bark split into smooth, thin splints.

GRASSES AND STEMS

Beach Grass—(Eastern Coast as far as N. and S. Carolina) Split white stems make coarse patterns in spruce root baskets.

Brome Grass—(Western Canada) Split white stems used for patterns in split root baskets.

Broom Corn—(Cultivated, mainly central West) Seed heads of broom corn and other sorghums are borne on long fine straw-like stems that make bundles for coiled baskets. Several strands laid side by side may take place of a flat weaver to be used for plaiting.

Cane—(Cultivated, southern states) Strips cut from outer stalk make flat plaiting material. Fine split strands used as weavers over spokes. A slight blow crushes the large grass-like stalk, the spongy pith is scraped away and the outer strips or splints are ready for use.

Galleta, or Black Bunch Grass—(Eastern and western U. S.) Stems used for foundations of coiled baskets.

Tufted Hairgrass—(Newfoundland to Alaska, south to New Jersey, Illinois, western mountains New Mexico, southern California) Split grass stems used for white pattern material in split root baskets.

Manna Grass—(Aquatic grass, swampy places of temperate regions) Split grass stems make white patterns in coiled baskets.

Red-top or Herd's Grass—(Eastern coast) Stems make good bundle material.

Red Milkweed, White Milkweed—(Scattered throughout U. S.) The stems of our common white species may be pounded until they separate into a mass of silky fibers easily twisted into a two-strand cord, used like sweet grass for weaving over splint spokes. The cord is strong enough to make knotted hammocks. Red and white milkweed twisted together, form a lovely tan and red rope. Shredded milkweed makes a soft foundation material for coiled baskets.

Reed Grass—(Scattered throughout U. S.) Tall slender stems split into strips for coiled basket patterns.

Wood Reed Grass or Indian Reed—(Shady places eastern and northern U. S.) Sections split from stem of grass woven into split root baskets to make white patterns.

Rice Grass—(Southern states) A tough grass excellent for coiled basketry, used like wire grass but of a coarser texture.

Basket Rush—(Throughout temperate regions) Flexible split stems used for plaited mats or baskets and for foundations or sewing material in coiled baskets. The varying natural colors of the stem are effective.

Bulrush, Cat-tail or Common Rush—(Scattered throughout U. S. in marshy places) Inner part of root stalk has a fibrous section, providing brown pattern material. Round stems are immersed several days in muddy water to darken them, forming black pattern material for basket bowls.

Sedge—(Scattered throughout U. S.) Long, tough, woody interior fibers of root stock used for white sewing strands of fine coiled baskets. Tough flexible grass-like stems make excellent bundle or sewing material.

Sweet Vernal Grass—(Cultivated eastern U. S.) Stems used as coiling foundations or weaving material. Grass strands make excellent foundation material for coiled baskets.

Tule—(Southwestern states) Slender rootlets dried and used for red or maroon patterns in twined weaving. Narrow strips from surface of stem twisted into long threads for finer twined baskets. Bark offers lovely green and brown shades used a great deal in making mats. Stems, whole or split, used for large baskets.

Wire Grass, Canadian Blue Grass—(Canada west to Nebraska, south to Virginia, Alabama, from northern California to British Columbia) A long grass growing wild in lowland meadows and swampy places, often to a height of three or four feet. Having neither ribs, nodules, branches nor blossoms, it has become so popular as a basketry material that it is sold in reed factories. Stems used in clumps for foundations of coiled baskets.

LEAVES

Agave—(Native to southern U. S.) Leaf fibers freed from soft tissue, make flexible material for starting baskets.

Cat-Tail—(Temperate and tropical regions) Leaves used entire for braiding. Slender ribbons split from tough part of leaves used flat or twisted as weavers. Bundles of split leaves make foundations for coiled baskets.

Holygrass Leaves—(Canada, northen U. S.) Long sweet-scented leaves twisted or braided for fine weaving strands, or used in bundles for coiling foundations.

Devil's Horn—(Western U. S.) Long green pod separates into two dark horns split into fine strips to make patterns in coiled baskets.

Iris—(Throughout U. S.) Brown dry leaf for coiling foundation, or when split into narrow strips, for weaving.

Palm Leaves—(Southern U. S.) Strips for plaiting cut from the flat, fibrous leaves. For fine work fleshy part of leaf is stripped away, leaving tough leaf-stalk for weaving or sewing.

Squaw Grass or Xerophyllum—(North America) Long, tough, lustrous leaves white, shaded a faint purple at one end, used for patterns in coiled baskets with lovely effect.

Sotol—(Southwestern U. S. deserts) Leaves split into strands ¼ inch wide, their harsh teeth removed, used in making twilled baskets.

Banana Yucca—(Arid southwestern U. S.) Split leaves, a delicate tone, used in strips to make plaited or twilled baskets, or in bundles for foundations of coiled baskets. Crimson roots used to make basket patterns.

Plains Yucca—(Arid southwestern U. S.) Greenish-yellow leaves split, used to make plaited or twilled baskets. Split into narrow strips they make flexible sewing strands. Strip leaves from their clusters at base of plant at any time of year. Use green or keep in a damp place until ready for use, wrap in a moist towel. Dry Yucca leaf baskets, then coat them with shellac.

FERNS

Giant Chain Fern—(Eastern half U. S. and southern Canada) Leaves removed, stalk of frond split into two slender, flat strands, making flexible and leathery weavers.

Maidenhair Fern—(Nova Scotia to British Columbia, southern mountains to Georgia and Arkansas) Slender, purplish-black stems, of glossy texture, split to make strands for weaving black designs in coiled baskets.

Goldenback Fern—(New Brunswick to N. Carolina and Tennessee) Black stem used as a substitute for maidenhair, which it resembles.

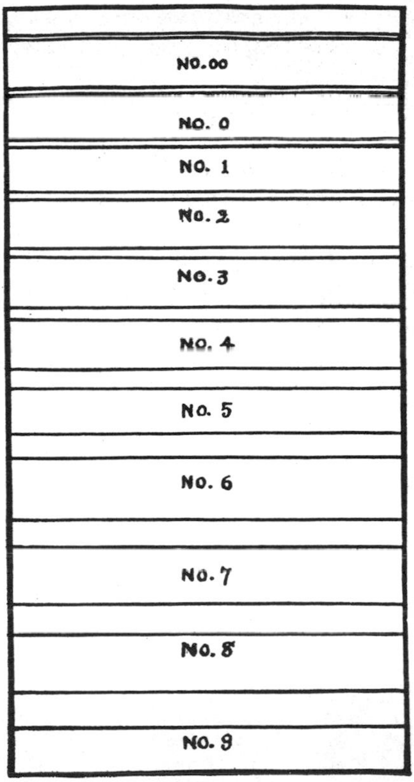

No.00

No. 0

No. 1

No. 2

No. 3

No. 4

No. 5

No. 6

No. 7

No. 8

No. 9

FIGURE 75—REED SIZES APPLIED TO
BASKETRY MATERIALS THROUGH-
OUT THE BOOK

INDEX